Athlone French Poets

GERARD DE NERVAL
Les Chimères

Athlone French Poets

General Editor EILEEN LE BRETON
Reader in French Language and Literature,
Bedford College University of London

MONOGRAPHS

Verlaine *by C. Chadwick*

Gérard de Nerval *by Norma Rinsler*

Saint-John Perse *by Roger Little*

CRITICAL EDITIONS

Paul Valéry: Charmes ou Poèmes
edited by Charles G. Whiting

Paul Verlaine: Sagesse
edited by C. Chadwick

Gérard de Nerval: Les Chimères
edited by Norma Rinsler

Saint-John Perse: Exil
edited by Roger Little

GERARD DE NERVAL

Les Chimères

edited by

NORMA RINSLER

UNIVERSITY OF LONDON
THE ATHLONE PRESS
1973

Published by
THE ATHLONE PRESS
UNIVERSITY OF LONDON
at 4 Gower Street, London WC1

Distributed by
Tiptree Book Services Ltd
Tiptree, Essex

U.S.A. and Canada
Humanities Press Inc
New York

© *Norma Rinsler*, 1973

0 485 14702 5 *cloth*
0 485 12702 4 *paperback*

Printed in Great Britain by
The Garden City Press Limited
Letchworth, Hertfordshire
SG6 1JS

Athlone French Poets

General Editor EILEEN LE BRETON

This series is designed to provide students and general readers both with Monographs of important nineteenth- and twentieth-century French poets and Critical Editions of representative works by these poets.

The Monographs aim at presenting the essential biographical facts while placing the poet in his social and intellectual context. They contain a detailed analysis of his poetical works and, where appropriate, a brief account of his other writings. His literary reputation is examined and his contribution to the development of French poetry is assessed, as is also his impact on other literatures. A selection of critical views and a bibliography are appended.

The Critical Editions contain a substantial introduction aimed at presenting each work against its historical background as well as studying its genre, structure, themes, style, etc. and highlighting its relevance for today. The text given is the complete text of the original edition. It is followed by full commentaries on the poems and annotation of the text, including variant readings when these are of real significance, and a select bibliography.

E. Le B.

CONTENTS

NOTE

All references to Nerval's works and correspondence are, except where otherwise indicated, to the edition in the Bibliothèque de la Pléiade, edited by Albert Béguin and Jean Richer, volume I (3rd edition, 1960) and volume II (1956). So as to avoid excessive numbers of footnotes, references to these volumes will be given in the text, in both Introduction and Commentaries, by title of work, volume number and page number; thus a quotation from *Sylvie* in the text will be followed by the reference (*Sylvie*; I, 241), or where the source has already been indicated, by volume and page number alone (I, 241).

The reference 'O.C.' is to the *Œuvres Complémentaires* edited by Jean Richer (Minard, *Lettres Modernes*):

O.C. I   volume I, *La Vie des Lettres*, 1959.
O.C. II   volume II, *La Vie du Théâtre*, 1961.
O.C. III   volume III, *Théâtre—(Piquillo et Les Monténégrins)*, 1965.
O.C. V   volume V, *L'Imagier de Harlem*, 1967.
O.C. VIII volume VIII, *Variétés et Fantaisies*, 1964.

INTRODUCTION

The writing of *Les Chimères* appears to extend over ten years of Gérard de Nerval's career, from 1844 to 1854. The first of these poems to be published was 'Le Christ aux Oliviers' (1844), followed by 'Vers Dorés' and 'Delfica' (1845). In 1853, these three poems were grouped together in *Petits Châteaux de Bohême* under the title *Mysticisme*, but no new ones were added to the group. In December 1853, 'El Desdichado' appeared, and at the end of January 1854, all the sonnets were published together under the title of *Les Chimères*, in the volume called *Les Filles du Feu*. About a fortnight later, 'Myrtho' was published separately.

We must beware of assuming that the publication dates of the sonnets are related directly to their dates of composition. In 1853 only the three poems already published eight or nine years earlier were included in *Petits Châteaux de Bohême*, but that does not necessarily mean that Nerval wrote no more of the group during the interval, and we cannot infer that the five sonnets which do not appear in *Petits Châteaux de Bohême* were all written during 1853. Various problems of dating are raised by the existence of a manuscript in the private collection of M. Dumesnil de Gramont, which contains six sonnets: 'à Madame Aguado', 'à Madame Ida Dumas', 'à Hélène de Mecklembourg' (subtitled 'Fontaine-bleau, mai 1837'), 'à J-y Colonna', 'à Louise d'Or Reine', 'à Madame Sand'. These appear under the title *Autres Chimères* in the Pléiade edition (I, 10–13). Three of these sonnets present versions of *Les Chimères* as we know them: 'à J-y Colonna' is composed, with minor variants, of the quatrains of the present 'Delfica' and the tercets of the present 'Myrtho' (see commentary on 'Delfica'); the final tercet of 'à Madame Aguado' is a variant of the final tercet of the present 'Delfica'; 'à Louise d'Or Reine' is substantially the same poem as the present 'Horus' (see commentary on 'Horus' and note 105). A second manuscript in the same collection, published in *Poésies de Gérard de Nerval*, ed. Pelletan (1924), contains one sonnet, entitled 'Myrtho', which is composed of the quatrains of the present 'Myrtho' and the tercets of the present 'Delfica' (see I, 12). Whatever the actual dates of these two manuscripts, it is clear that an early version of 'Horus' existed at the same time as the early partial version of 'Delfica'; thus 'Horus', first published in 1854, appears to have been conceived not later than 1845, when 'Delfica' was published. The same is evidently true of at least the tercets of 'Myrtho'; while the quatrains, which appear on the second manuscript together with the 1845 version of the tercets of 'Delfica', must have been written in the same period.

The sonnet 'Antéros', of which no manuscript version has been found, introduces, alongside its references to classical mythology, an element of Biblical reference not to be found in 'Delfica', 'Myrtho' and 'Horus'. This element is not altogether new, for 'Le Christ aux Oliviers' mingles Biblical and classical references in a deliberate synthesis. In 'Antéros' however the Biblical images are predominant, and the figure of Jehovah has a more remote, more powerfully disturbing quality than the figures of Kneph, Isis or Iacchus, or the company of 'les dieux'. The tone of this sonnet is correspondingly less detached and reflective. The same emotional climate is to be found in the story of Adoniram in *Voyage en Orient*, especially in the account of Adoniram's visit to the home of his ancestors, the children of Cain. The *Carnet de Notes du Voyage en Orient* shows that in 1843, Nerval had already noted the equivalence of Greek, Roman and Egyptian gods[1]; the same notebook contains jottings relating to the race of Cain. Although Adoniram's story was not published until 1850, the germ of the sonnet may belong to the period of the journey itself, that is to 1843–4, especially as the theme of 'Antéros' links it closely with 'Delfica', 'Myrtho' and 'Horus'. On the other hand, it may well have been written at the later date; another text published in 1850 (*Le Diable rouge*; II, 1215–9) is much concerned with Milton's Lucifer and with Prometheus, who both contributed something to 'Antéros'.

We are left with 'El Desdichado' and 'Artémis', of which manuscript versions do exist. However, since the two sonnets always appear together, it is difficult to decide how early or late in Nerval's career they may have been written. One of these manuscripts contains a third sonnet called 'Erythréa', an alternative version of the sonnet 'A Madame Aguado', which itself appears

on the manuscript containing the early versions of 'Horus' and
'Delfica' (and has tercets from which those of the present 'Delfica'
are derived);[2] but no firm conclusions about the dates of 'El
Desdichado' and 'Artémis' can be drawn from this, for it is
possible that Nerval was simply re-copying an earlier sonnet
which seemed to him to have some connection with the later
ones. There are links between 'Artémis' and the play *L'Imagier de
Harlem*, which was produced in 1851 (see commentary on
'Artémis'), but we have no way of knowing which was written
first: the play may be reflecting the sonnet, or the sonnet the play;
or they may have been written at about the same time. We have
in fact no documentary evidence to show that 'El Desdichado'
and 'Artémis' were not also the product of the earlier period, and
withheld from publication like 'Horus', 'Antéros' and 'Myrtho'.
Only their greater density leads one to imagine that they are the
product of a period nearer the end of the poet's life.

If we cannot draw definite conclusions about the time of
composition of most of these sonnets, we can however observe
certain intentions implicit in their author's treatment of them. It
is evident that he thought of 'Le Christ aux Oliviers', 'Vers
Dorés' and 'Delfica' as belonging together, since they were
published as a group, under a common title, in 1853. 'Myrtho'
appears to have close links with 'Delfica', yet it was not put into
the same group. 'Horus', although it was substantially complete
at a time when 'Delfica' was still not disentangled from 'Myrtho',
was not published at all until 1854. For long periods of his life
Nerval was desperately short of copy and very anxious to con-
vince his contemporaries of his continued ability to write; there
must therefore have been compelling reasons for not publishing
'Myrtho' and 'Horus' earlier; and those reasons may equally
apply to 'Antéros', 'Artémis' and 'El Desdichado'. There is a
strong possibility that in publishing 'El Desdichado' without
Nerval's permission, Alexandre Dumas may have forced his
friend's hand, and that Nerval had intended never to publish the
remaining sonnets at all. One final conclusion may be drawn: the
fact that the twelve sonnets ultimately appeared together under a
common title indicates that Nerval intended them to be seen as
a group, as a single work in fact; and further, their appearance in
the volume containing *Les Filles du Feu* suggests that they are

probably connected in some way with his prose writings in that volume.

If *Les Chimères* does indeed form a coherent whole, it should be immediately obvious that the work must be read as a whole, and interpreted as a whole. It has been common practice, in studying these poems, to make certain assumptions about their relations to each other. Both 'Le Christ aux Oliviers' and 'Vers Dorés' have generally been regarded as standing apart from the rest, as from each other, and have rarely been included in a study of the whole group; 'Delfica' and 'Myrtho' are usually seen as alternative versions of the same poem; 'Horus' and 'Antéros' are sometimes treated as if they bore no relation to *Les Chimères* as a whole, or to *Les Filles du Feu*, and are grouped together on stylistic grounds, because both seem to have a 'Parnassian' quality;[3] 'Artémis' on the contrary is admired for its apparently inscrutable mystery, when it is not regarded as frankly incoherent; 'El Desdichado', the most famous of all, has evident links with 'Delfica' and 'Myrtho', since the same images may be found in all three, but beyond pointing to these echoes, commentators have generally preferred to treat 'El Desdichado' as if it stood alone. Reference is often made, as one would expect, to *Les Filles du Feu*. Of these, *Octavie* is obviously related to 'Delfica' and to 'Myrtho', and thus in part to 'El Desdichado', while *Isis* may throw some light on 'Horus', in which the goddess Isis is named. Some aspects of the sonnets, as of all Nerval's work, are related by some commentators to events in the poet's life, and most frequently to his love for the actress Jenny Colon, of which a fictional account is given in *Sylvie*, and, in part, in *Corilla*. Certain themes and images in the sonnets (for example, the *étoile* and the *rose trémière*) occur in the visions recounted in *Aurélia*. An alternative name for Aurélia, as we know from the manuscript of *La Pandora* (I, 1261, n. 1 to p. 348), was Artémis; and a manuscript note which refers to the tale of Brisacier (used by Nerval in the preface to *Les Filles du Feu*) bears the title *Aurélia* (I, 1220). It would appear that Nerval intended at first to tell the story of Brisacier and the actress he calls his 'froide étoile' as a separate section of *Les Filles du Feu*. But we have only the fragment which found its way into the preface, though more light is cast on the story by *Sylvie*; and the name of *Aurélia* was transferred to a work which is not merely the story of an unhappy love. It seems indisputable that there are links between that work and *Les Chimères*. There is however an essential difference between the tone of *Aurélia* and that of *Octavie*, of *Sylvie*, and, to an even more marked degree, of *Les Chimères*. Where *Aurélia* attempts a direct transcription and examination of the poet's experience, offering us a frank account of his problems and his dreams (though ordered and expressed, and in part mytho-logized, by a consummate artist), *Les Chimères*, like *Octavie* and especially *Sylvie*, is a total transformation of experience. The dreams and visions of *Aurélia* seem sometimes to tell us more than Nerval may have realised; but *Les Chimères*, like *Sylvie*, is a work of art in which the poet says, as exactly as possible, what he has chosen to express; as long as Nerval felt that the sonnets said too much, or did not say it acceptably, he did not publish them. Thus, though we are at liberty to use the confidences of *Aurélia* to throw light on *Les Chimères*, the sonnets should be regarded first and foremost as a complete and coherent work of art which must be read as it stands.

But how are we to read them? Because of their difficulty, there has been a constant tendency to regard *Les Chimères* either as 'hermetic', that is as enshrining some occult message, or alterna-tively, as we shall see, as 'pure poetry', despite the view of Aristide Marie, his first scholarly biographer, that Nerval was '(un) classique, pénétré de claire tradition'.[4] Nerval did not consider himself sufficiently important to issue a manifesto, and in any case his contemporaries did not regard him primarily as a poet. His views on poetry are therefore expressed in a rather fragmentary fashion, in comments on other people's work and ideas, and at greatest length in his studies of folk-poetry, 'Sur les Chansons populaires' (1850-2) and *Chansons et Légendes du Valois* (appended to *Sylvie* in *Les Filles du Feu*, 1854, but the earliest version of the text dates from 1842). All these various writings make it plain that he is no advocate of 'pure poetry', and would probably not have accepted that the term has any meaning. He values freshness of feeling much more highly than technical accomplishment, and is inclined to suspect that perfection of form conceals a lack of genuine passion. In the Preface to his translation of Goethe's *Second Faust* (1840),[5] he approves Goethe's view of the relative importance of form and content in poetry, describing Goethe's opinion as 'la critique d'une certaine poésie de mots plutôt que d'idées': his quotation is from Goethe's *Dichtung und Wahrheit*: 'ce qu'il y a de plus important, de fondamental, ce qui produit l'impression la plus profonde, ce qui agit avec le plus d'efficacité sur notre moral dans une œuvre poétique, c'est ce qui reste du poète dans une traduction en prose . . .' (O.C. I, 24). In a passionate defence of creative adventurousness, Nerval's Adoniram, in *Voyage en Orient* (II, 513), exalts the power of the symbolic image, and refuses to accord any value to 'les vulgarités de la forme', which merely create the empty shell of a work of art. In itself, perfection of form has no value; it must be the outward expression of an inner compulsion. In Heine's work, says Nerval approvingly, 'l'idée et la forme s'identifient complètement' (O.C. I, 75). The form is the incarnation of the idea. For Nerval, the rhythms and images of his art were secondary to the meaning he had to convey. Gautier remarked that his friend 's'occupait plus de l'idée que de l'image';[6] and Nerval himself asked 'où est le vers? . . . dans la mesure, dans la rime,—ou dans l'idée?' ('Sur les Chansons populaires'; I, 466).[7]

Nerval would not have shared the view that poetry is the prerogative of an elite, and he repeatedly insists on its links with everyday existence. He regrets the fact that in France 'la littérature n'est jamais descendue au niveau de la grande foule' (*Chansons et Légendes du Valois*; I, 276). Language was made for communication; and the poet ought not to talk down to the rest of mankind: Nerval deplores the Olympian aloofness of Goethe's attitude to others, his 'glaciale impartialité'; and he commends the humanity and warmth of Heine. His praise of Heine's *Intermezzo* (which he translated with superb understanding) tells us much about his own view of what poetry should be (O.C. I, 85–8):

une suite de petites pièces isolées et marquées par des numéros, qui, sans avoir de liaison apparente entre elles, se rattachent à la même idée . . . Toutes ces strophes décousues ont une unité,—l'amour. C'est là un amour entièrement inédit—non qu'il ait rien de singulier, car chacun y reconnaîtra son histoire; ce qui fait sa nouveauté, c'est qu'il est vieux comme le monde, et les choses qu'on dit les dernières sont les choses naturelles . . . Voilà des accents et des touches dignes de Salomon, le premier écrivain qui ait confondu dans le même lyrisme le sentiment de l'amour et le sentiment de Dieu . . . toute l'âme humaine vibre dans ces petites pièces . . . il y a çà et là des pensées de moraliste condensées en deux vers, en deux mots . . . En lisant l'*Intermezzo*, l'on éprouve comme une espèce d'effroi: vous rougissez comme surpris dans votre secret . . . Il semble que le poète ait entendu vos sanglots, et pourtant ce sont les siens qu'il a notés.

The true expression of emotion is only a beginning. Human emotion is not the sum total of human experience. The emotion must be seen in its proper context, in the context of the whole natural world, so that it becomes clear to the reader that the poet is expressing not only 'le sentiment de l'amour' but also 'le sentiment de Dieu' (O.C. I, 89):

Comme tous les grands poètes, Heine a toujours la nature présente. Dans sa rêverie la plus abstraite, sa passion la plus abîmée en elle-même ou sa mélancolie la plus désespérée, une image, une épithète formant tableau, vous rappellent ce changeant et mobile paysage qui vous entoure sans cesse, éternelle décoration du drame humain. —Cet amour ainsi exhalé au milieu des formes, des couleurs et des sons, vivant de la vie générale, malgré l'égoïsme naturel à la passion, emprunte à l'imagination panthéiste du poète une grandeur facile et simple qu'on ne rencontre pas ordinairement chez les rimeurs élégiaques.

The poet must also be able to generalise ('des pensées de mora-liste') from his personal experience, which is not essentially different from, still less superior to, the experience of any man: 'La vie d'un poète est celle de tous' (*Petits Châteaux de Bohême*; I, 65). The poet is distinguished only by his gift of words, which enables him to give striking expression to what is generally apprehended only vaguely in daily life. By so doing, he may add to the store of human understanding: 'l'expérience de chacun est le trésor de tous' (*Promenades et Souvenirs*; I, 133). This point of view implies a belief in the utility of poetry which is hardly consistent with an attempt to create 'pure poetry'. 'Tout ce qui est utile est laid', remarks Gautier firmly. His friend Nerval, on the contrary, repeatedly expresses the hope that his work will be a useful record of one man's experience.[8] His reservations in *Aurélia* are typical (I, 364):

Si je ne pensais que la mission d'un écrivain est d'analyser sincèrement ce qu'il éprouve dans les graves circonstances de la vie, et si je ne me proposais un but que je crois utile, je m'arrêterais ici . . .

It is the desire to be of some use to his fellow-men that lies behind his joyful transcription of his vision of love triumphant over death, at the end of *Aurélia*: 'C'est alors que je suis descendu parmi les hommes pour leur annoncer l'heureuse nouvelle' (I, 410).

Now if the poet is to speak to others of matters which concern them equally, he will presumably try to speak a language which others can understand. However difficult *Les Chimères* may appear to be, we must infer that Nerval did not set out to evoke the rare and esoteric for its own sake. On the contrary, he strove constantly for clarity and precision, and it was such 'classical' qualities that his contemporaries praised in his work. Baudelaire thought him 'doué d'une intelligence brillante, active, lumineuse', and his numerous writings 'tous marqués par le goût'.[9] Heine found in his style 'une pureté suave'.[10] Gautier remarked that 'peu de littérateurs de notre temps ont une langue plus châtiée, plus nette et plus transparente . . .', and later added that 'Le style de Gérard était une lampe qui apportait la lumière dans les ténèbres de la pensée et du mot'.[11] Nerval himself was troubled by the obscurity of Goethe's *Second Faust*: he notes in the preface to his translation of this work that it was not understood by many of its readers in Germany, and apologises for not having succeeded in making his French version any more accessible than the original (O.C. I, 23–4):

nous regrettons de n'avoir pu y répandre peut-être toute la clarté désirable. La pensée même de l'auteur est souvent abstraite et voilée comme à dessein, et l'on est forcé alors d'en donner l'interprétation plutôt que le sens. C'est ce défaut capital, surtout pour le lecteur français, qui nous a obligé de remplacer par une analyse quelques parties accessoires du nouveau *Faust*.

We may assume that in his own work Nerval would try to avoid what he considered a 'défaut capital' in others. If the sonnets sometimes appear obscure, it is not because Nerval is trying to create difficulties for the reader, but because they are the embodiment of ideas and feelings of an extremely complex nature, which do not lend themselves to expression in simple terms. In addition, what appears to be obscurity is frequently understatement, which may make considerable demands on the reader's imagination. As Albert Béguin remarked (I, xvi), Nerval possessed the singular virtue of being determined to 'ne jamais prononcer un mot plus haut qu'il ne fallait'. In no sense, however, can it be claimed that Nerval is a 'mystificateur'.

The question of Nerval's madness has, of course, influenced interpretation of *Les Chimères*, as of *Aurélia*. Gautier glossed over the difficulty of the sonnets by underlining the evident artistry which had gone to make their form: 'L'étrangeté la plus inouie se revêt, chez Gérard de Nerval, de formes pour ainsi dire classiques'.[12] It might possibly be argued that the content of the sonnets is irrational, and this could then be explained in one of two ways: either the poet offers us (probably without realising it) glimpses into the hidden recesses of the human mind, or he is a visionary who sees with full consciousness further into the mysteries of Creation than ordinary mortals see. In the first case, we may try to approach him with the methods of psychological analysis (and this has been attempted by, for instance, L.-H. Sebillotte and Ch. Mauron—see note 21). In the second case, we can only follow at a distance and admire; in doing so we may rejoin, ultimately, the notion that *Les Chimères* is 'pure poetry', which speaks of the ineffable, or we may be tempted to interpret the visionary's message according to our own religious or esoteric preferences.

In the preface to *Les Filles du Feu*, Nerval himself wrote of his sonnets: 'Ils ne sont guère plus obscurs que la métaphysique d'Hégel ou les *Mémorables* de Swedenborg, et perdraient de leur charme à être expliqués, si la chose était possible . . .' In one sense at least he was right: over the years the sonnets have many times been stripped of their magical effect, their *charme*, by inappropriate explanation or interpretation. We may turn to the poet himself for a hint of the right way: 'concédez-moi du moins le mérite de l'expression' (I, 159). This does not mean that the sonnets are only a beautiful arrangement of words, but that Nerval believed that he had expressed his thoughts, so far as he was able, in the most appropriate way. Paraphrase or 'explanation' may make a poem clearer, but we must remember that even if it is appropriate it will be much less powerful than the poem.

The fact still remains that if one sets aside the 'pure poetry' hypothesis, most readers of *Les Chimères* find the text extremely difficult of access. Nerval's contemporaries did not publish any interpretations of his poems; they regarded them as impenetrable, and possibly insane, though certainly possessing 'le mérite de l'expression'. The Symbolist critics regarded them as mysterious in the best possible way, a 'chant sybillin', in the words of Henri de Régnier, whose meaning was not to be spelled out, but divined through its 'harmonieuse incantation'.[13] Some modern critics still resist the notion that the sonnets can be understood: Albert Béguin affirmed in 1936 that 'toutes les tentatives d'intrusion logique sont restées vaines',[14] and this is echoed twenty years later by E. Aunos, who concludes from the multiplicity of the sonnets' possible meanings that we can never know their secret.[15] Yves Le Dantec doubts if we would enjoy the sonnets more if we possessed all their 'clefs',[16] and Gilbert Rouger advises us simply to listen to their music.[17] Since the mid-twentieth century, however, the interpreters have occupied most of the territory, and particularly since the centenary, in 1955, of Nerval's death. The spate of Nerval criticism since then has been adroitly and wittily analysed by Raymond Jean (himself a perceptive critic of Nerval), in an article wearily entitled 'Encore Nerval'.[18] He applauds the recent attempt to return to the text, and deplores the 'délires d'exégèse, déchiffrements forcenés, systématisations maniaques' which have made of Nerval's work merely 'un objet *d'interprétation*'. Raymond Jean classifies contemporary criticism of Nerval under the following headings 'selon un ordre de *formalisme* décroissant': *l'occultisme*—which includes all explanation of the sonnets with reference to alchemy, astrology and the Tarot, as in the work of G. Le Breton and Jean Richer;[19] *l'esotérisme*—which is historical and bibliographical in method (and of which Jean comments that it is an inexhaustible source of new material 'pour peu que l'érudition s'y applique', adding that 'Elle le fait en général avec entrain'); then *la symbolique spiritualiste*, which relates the sonnets to familiar patterns of religious myth, and of which the sensitive explorations of François Constans[20] are an example; *la crypto-psychologie*, as practised by L.-H. Sebillotte and Ch. Mauron (and of which, Jean seems to feel, the less said the better);[21] and finally, *la psychanalyse littéraire*, Jungian rather than Freudian in method, which includes the work of such writers as J.-P. Richard.[22]

Faced with this divergence of opinion, it is tempting to revert to the notion that we would be wise not to worry too much about the meaning of these sonnets. But even the most superficial reading reveals at once that one cannot regard them as essays in the creation of musical sound. There is a tough core of intractable meaning in them which one cannot ignore, and an anguished tone which is not conducive to comfortably passive 'appreciation'.

The greatest danger of interpretation, and the common fault of the 'systématisations' which Raymond Jean condemns, is that it may lead one away from the sonnets themselves. Instead of examining the structure which the poet created, the critic may be tempted to fit the sonnets into a pre-existing structure of his own. To this end, he will often limit his operations to one, or perhaps two, of the sonnets, thus disrupting what Nerval himself regarded as the essential unity of the group: 'il faut que vous les entendiez tous' (I, 158). The present study intends to propose that coherence is the first essential in an account of *Les Chimères*, and that all attempts to give such an account must begin and end with the text itself. The meaning of any one sonnet must be understood in relation to the group as a whole. Beyond this, it will sometimes be necessary to link the sonnets with other works by Nerval, poetry or prose, since the poet's own conception of his images can often be illuminated by reference to other works of his in which they appear. Few writers, I think, can have produced a body of work in which the separate items are so closely related to each other. Poems, stories, critical studies and essays, widely separated in time and apparently differing widely in scope and context, offer the reader the same recurrent images, the same themes, the same preoccupations. In effect, Nerval wrote only one work, which is essentially the story of his life, 'l'histoire du cœur d'un grand poète'; every part of it sheds some light on every other part. Elucidation from within the poet's own work is thus to be preferred, wherever possible, to that which looks outside it; what matters is the meaning his words had for Nerval himself. External references will of course be noted if they seem to help, but the dangers of too much exegesis are on the whole greater than those of too little. Despite his reputation for eclecticism, Nerval was not a random collector of unrelated trifles, and his borrowings and allusions always reflect a small number of intensely important private concerns. Since these concerns are, as he freely admitted, common to the greater part of mankind ('la vie d'un poète est celle de tous'), it is reasonable to suppose that his references, however remote from us they appear at first sight, are grouped about a central community of ideas in which the reader can share. Moreover, unless a reference conveys something general and familiar to the reader, it is unlikely to make its effect *as a reference*, that is, as a recognisable reminder of something else; and that 'something else' will then be irrelevant to the working of the poem and to the reader's understanding of it. 'Ils ne sont guère plus obscurs que la métaphysique d'Hégel ou les *Mémorables* de Swedenborg . . .'; does the poet not mean to point out to us that there are some things which cannot be said in words of one syllable, but that these things are accessible to those who will learn to read them?

It must be remembered, however, that the modern reader of *Les Chimères* is at a disadvantage. The averagely cultured reader in Nerval's time, and particularly if he belonged to Nerval's own generation, was almost certainly in possession of a wider knowledge of classical literature, myth and legend than the averagely well-educated English reader of today. In addition, those who were likely to read the journals in which some of Nerval's poems first appeared would have had a good acquaintance with the literature of their own times, English and German as well as French. References which seem obscure to us may well have seemed perfectly clear to Nerval's contemporaries.

SOURCES

It would be difficult, and perhaps not altogether profitable, to compile a list of all the possible sources of the ideas, vocabulary and imagery of *Les Chimères*; and most difficult of all, to know where to stop. A list of sources which stretches to include such fundamental ingredients of European culture as the Bible and Homer, can serve no useful purpose beyond reminding us that the writer in question is a product of a European culture: though that is an essential beginning. It is almost misleading in Nerval's case to speak of sources at all, in the usual sense. Nerval accumulated, throughout his life, sometimes in notebooks but more often in his memory, a great store of material, some from his actual experience, some from the books he read, and some imagined. He took, from whatever source, only what might serve his purpose, and as soon as he had taken it, it was transformed. There is no external scale of values which can decide what an artist may choose to work with; what is entirely insignificant or lacking in dignity in other men's eyes, may offer him just what he needs. Nerval had an endless curiosity about people, and frequented with equally passionate interest the salons of the great and the bars of Montmartre. In the same way, he was interested in all forms of literature and art, and especially in the theatre, where his enthusiasm was equally roused by high tragedy, operetta, grand opera and puppet-show. His affection for particular writers and works was, like his predilection for certain towns and landscapes, based on his personal concerns, so that he often cherished for himself what his critical judgement correctly perceived to be inferior as art.

Many lesser writers contributed something to Nerval's stock of images, and there are literally hundreds of echoes to be found in his pages—to speak only of those whose origin has been recognised. Here again, it is important to remember that what matters is the significance a particular image, or a name, had for the poet himself; and it is often of little consequence whether we recognise the allusion as an allusion or not. It is doubtful, in most cases, whether they are meant as allusions at all, in the sense that, for instance, T. S. Eliot's references to Dante are: Eliot means us to think of Dante (if we are sufficiently well-read to recognise his intention); Nerval does not mean us to think of his minor authors, but of those central preoccupations which made him remember their images, and which, he believed, he shared with his reader in their widest implications, if not in particular detail. To take one example: M. Léon Cellier has pointed out that the sonnet 'Artémis' contains what appear to be references to Meyerbeer's opera *Robert le Diable* (for which Scribe wrote the libretto);[23] Robert may also be the 'duc normand' of 'Myrtho'. It would be pointless to expend ingenuity on tracing further links between 'Artémis' and *Robert le Diable*, and one would not be at much of a disadvantage if one came to 'Artémis' without ever having heard of *Robert le Diable*. The opera was a tremendously popular spectacle which Nerval obviously enjoyed; but whatever he took

from it in writing 'Artémis' has been made entirely new, and
belongs now to 'Artémis', and not to Scribe. One might say
indeed that Nerval was only taking what was already his own,
that it was because he was potentially the poet of 'Artémis' that
the images of *Robert le Diable* struck him with such force. Jung
remarks that the human mind assimilates only those experiences
which accord with its own predisposition: 'It is not as if the
impressions pressed haphazard upon us, it is our own disposition
which supplies the condition for the impression'.[24]

What is most interesting is the extent to which literature acted,
for Nerval, as a mirror to his own life. It is often difficult to
disentangle his real experience from his literary experience;
memories of real people and places become fused with remi-
niscences of books read, or plays and operas seen in the theatre.
Often one feels that the real experience took its tone from a
literary model, or is remembered because of a literary echo. He
was one of those men who are so sensitive to the power of language
that nothing seems real until it has been successfully put into
words, and anything which has been successfully put into words
seems real. He recognised this trait in himself: 'J'aime à conduire
ma vie comme un roman' (*Voyage en Orient*; II, 342);[25] the
experience he has gathered from other men's books influences
his view of his own experience. Conversely, as we have seen,
certain works of literature are remembered and remarked on
solely because they remind the poet of his own life, so that his
accounts of Heine, or of Restif de la Bretone, tell us as much about
Nerval himself as they do about Heine and Restif. When he
comes to write books of his own, he turns naturally to his own
experience for material: 'Je suis du nombre des écrivains dont la
vie tient intimement aux ouvrages qui les ont fait connaître'
(*Promenades et Souvenirs*; I, 139). He has been accused of lacking
invention, but he was one of those whose only material is their
own substance: 'Inventer, au fond, c'est se ressouvenir', he said
(Preface, *Les Filles du Feu*; I, 150–1). It will be evident that the
word must be taken in its widest sense; it does not mean that his
accounts of his experience, whether in prose or in verse, are
strictly factual accounts of 'real' events. 'Se ressouvenir' includes
remembering the experiences one has heard about or imagined,
and the books one has read. Nerval could be caught up in his

own inventions, too, so that the feelings he created for his characters, out of his own experience and other men's accounts of theirs, became as real to him as his own responses to reality: 'on arrive pour ainsi dire à s'incarner dans le héros de son imagination, si bien que sa vie devienne la vôtre et qu'on brûle des flammes factices de ses ambitions et de ses amours!' (Ibid.; I, 150). It becomes hard to say with any certainty what is fact and what is imagination. In one sense at least it is all 'fact': it all happened to Nerval, whether materially or imaginatively, and is therefore all equally relevant to an understanding of his poetry.

Besides the events of his life (which are telescoped and re-ordered according to the demands of the work they help to form), two elements in particular appear to contribute to Nerval's stock of poetic material: classical literature, both Greek and Roman, and German literature, especially the *Faust* of Goethe and the poems of Heine. It is typical of him that he should look for points of contact between these apparently diverse worlds. He did not subscribe to the view of Mme de Staël that there was an opposition between 'ancient' and 'modern' literature; there were no 'dead' cultures for Nerval, as there were no dead gods, and classical litera-ture was the voice of a paradisal Golden Age which he believed to be still accessible. When he encountered German Romantic litera-ture, he placed it alongside the classical works he had studied earlier, and saw at once in his favourite German writers the effects of a classical heritage. He described Goethe as embracing both the classical and the modern eras: 'il faut remarquer que Goethe n'admet guère d'idées qui n'aient pas une base dans la poésie classique, si neuves que soient, d'ailleurs, sa forme et sa pensée de détail' (O.C. I, 19). Similarly, he says of Heine 'Il est en effet Grec avant tout', and describes the characteristic movement of Heine's prose as being that of 'la période grecque, simple, coulante, facile à saisir, et aussi harmonieuse à l'oreille qu'à la vue' (O.C. I, 84). Nerval's contact with classical literature dates from his schooldays, and there is ample evidence that the Greek and Latin authors whose work he knew provided him with something more than a stock of literary ornaments: he uses them constantly as points of reference in judging modern writers, and they seem to embody for him a standard of excellence in the poetic expression of universal truths. He took from them also a whole series of images to mirror his own preoccupations; in so doing, he gave to his private experience the dignity and the timeless scope of myth. Far from aiming at a purely personal or an obscurely hermetic significance, he intended, by using these images, to make his account of his experience *less* private, more universally recognisable. Universality is a quality Nerval much admired in Heine, and he is careful to point out that it is an innate quality of the poet's mind, not a literary device. He speaks of Heine's 'imagination panthéiste' (O.C. I, 89), and of Goethe's 'système panthéistique' (O.C. I, 22), and there is a real difference between the two. Heine reaches an apprehension of the unity of nature through his imagination, intuitively; Goethe begins with the principle of unity and looks for the evidence. Of the two, it is Heine who is nearer to Nerval's own instincts: 'Heine n'a jamais créé de système, il est trop universel pour cela' (O.C. I, 85). We shall not then expect to find a *système* of any kind in Nerval's own work, but rather an attempt to seize with the imagination, and express in words, something which seems to him to be 'universel', something transcending individual differences and historical change, defying, as Faust does, the laws of time and space, and expressing, as Heine does, the most secret sufferings and joys of the human heart.

For all Nerval's explorations lead back to 'le monde interne'. He has been credited with being the first French poet to use the imagery of dreams and the resources of the unconscious in his work, and the Surrealists regarded *Aurélia* as the first Surrealist text. They were taking their cue in part, no doubt, from Nerval's description of the sonnets in the preface to *Les Filles du Feu*, as 'composés dans cet état de rêverie *supernaturaliste*, comme diraient les Allemands' (I, 158). The allied term 'surnaturaliste' was almost adopted by Apollinaire for his play *Les Mamelles de Tirésias*, which he finally designated 'drame surréaliste'. Nerval was not thinking however in terms of the Surrealists' 'merveilleux' or of Apollinaire's 'surprise', or of a 'stream of consciousness' technique, or indeed of any kind of *système*. By *rêverie* he means a meditative or contemplative state, in which the mind is both receptive to experience and actively organising experience.[26] In 'Cagliostro' (II, 1173) Nerval speaks of 'un certain esprit de mysticisme ou de supernaturalisme nécessaire aux imaginations rêveuses et délicates'. A 'Supernaturaliste' appears among the philosophers in the Walpurgisnachtstraum in Goethe's *Faust*, which Nerval translated in 1827–8, and the term 'Supernaturalist' occurs in the writings of Heine, some of whose works Nerval had translated. 'In art I am a Supernaturalist', says Heine; he pours scorn on art which is content with imitating what exists in nature, and insists that the true artist goes beyond nature to create symbolic images from the resources of his own mind.[27] A 'Supernaturalist' art is one which embodies both physical and spiritual realities, the visible world and 'le monde interne'. Nerval was aware that the world as it is experienced inside the mind, is composed of elements not wholly amenable to daylight reason; his vision of the unity of human experience, whether actual or imagined, led him to consider dreams and daydreams as an integral part of a man's life: 'Le rêve est une seconde vie', he wrote at the beginning of *Aurélia* (I, 359). But he did not see dreams as an escape from reality, or as a decorative device to broaden the scope of his imagery, and he was not attracted by the temptations of chaos. On the contrary, he sought for a comprehensive order, which would include the element of dream. Dream, it seemed to him, was a vital contact with the world, like that of waking attention, only it led the dreamer into areas of experience whose nature and logic he could not always understand: 'Je crus comprendre qu'il existait entre le monde externe et le monde interne un lien; que l'inattention ou le désordre d'esprit en faussaient seuls les rapports apparents' (I, 413). From this second life, 'où le moi, sous une autre forme, continue l'œuvre de l'existence', a man could learn much of importance if he could learn to 'read' his dreams. Those works of literature which attempt to transcribe visions he refers to as 'ces études de l'âme humaine' (I, 359); he is chiefly concerned with what may be learned from them of the workings of the human mind. He also felt that it ought to be possible to some extent to direct one's dreams, by preparing one's mind and ordering one's thoughts,[28] so that subsequently the dream would offer a logic nearer to waking logic, enabling the dreamer to understand its message more clearly. He was partly afraid of what his dreams might tell him, but determined not to neglect what he might learn from them: 'je m'encourageais à une audacieuse

tentative. Je résolus de fixer le rêve et d'en connaître le secret . . .'
(I, 412). Before he could learn the secret of dreams, and discover
how to control the effects of 'cette chimère attrayante et redout-
able', he had to learn to 'fixer le rêve'. This could only mean, for
a man with his horror of the constraining *système*, that he must
try to grasp with his imagination the logic of the dream, the
patterns of experience it revealed to him; and he must then fix
those patterns in words, constructing a logic within his poem
which would mirror the logic he glimpsed in the world of his
imagination. His fear was not without reason, for in that world,
as in any man's dreams, the laws of time and space by which we
order and measure our everyday behaviour are no longer
operative.[29] His description of dream as a *chimère* leads us directly
to the sonnets, in which we shall in fact find experience ordered,
not according to our everyday conceptions of time and space, but
according to the logic of the imagination.

THEMES

The title of *Les Chimères* is the first thing to be considered. It will
be remembered that some of these poems were published to-
gether in 1853, thus forming a sub-group as it were, under the
title *Mysticisme*. This heading evidently seemed no longer suitable
for the group as a whole. How did *Mysticisme* become *Les Chi-
mères*? The immediately obvious answer is that Nerval was aware
that between the three poems published in 1853, and the remain-
ing ones, there were links which justified grouping them all
together under the new title. Mysticism, like the themes of the
previously unpublished poems, was a *chimère*. What connotations
had this word for Nerval?

It appears in his work as early as 1827, in his first substantial
publication, *Elégies nationales et satires politiques*. Most of the poems
in this volume are inspired by the legend of Napoleon, but one or
two have a more personal (though essentially conventional)
theme. Among these is 'Ode':

> 'Illusions! vaines images! . . .
> Le bonheur n'est point sur la terre,
> Votre amour n'est qu'une chimère,
> Votre lyre n'a que des sons!'

The words are those of the level-headed citizens who would like to save the poet from disillusion. But he is not interested in their kind of truth:

> Ah! préférons cette chimère
> A leur froide moralité;
> Fuyons leur voix triste et sévère;
> Si le mal est réalité,
> Et si le bonheur est un songe,
> Fixons les yeux sur le mensonge,
> Pour ne pas voir la vérité . . .

The knowingly disillusioned tone of this poem is probably a reflection of currently fashionable attitudes, rather than the genuinely personal reaction to experience of a boy of nineteen who had led a sheltered life. The same disenchanted pose is evident in 'La Gloire', which rejects illusions of grandeur and fame, preferring the illusions of love:

> O chimère de l'homme! ô songe de la vie!
> O vaine illusion, d'illusions suivie!
> Qu'on parle de grandeur et d'immortalité . . .
> O vanité de l'homme! aveuglement stupide
> D'un atome perdu dans les déserts du vide . . .
> Choisissons donc au moins la plus aimable erreur,
> Celle qui nous promet un instant de douceur.
> Oh! viens me consoler, amour, belle chimère!

Both poems are summed up in the last lines of 'Pensée de Byron' (I, 21; this last verse was suppressed when the poem was reprinted in *Petits Châteaux de Bohême* in 1853):

> Trop longtemps épris d'un vain songe,
> Gloire! amour! vous eûtes mon cœur:
> O Gloire! tu n'es qu'un mensonge;
> Amour! tu n'es point le bonheur!

The words *chimère, mensonge, erreur*, are obviously equivalent; and the same meaning is attached to *chimère* in a poem which touches on the theme of religion, 'Prière de Socrate':

> Brûlant de te connaître, ô divin Créateur!
> J'analysai souvent les cultes de la terre,
> Et je ne vis partout que mensonge et chimère . . .

The implication in every case is that a *chimère* is an illusory good which men strive to attain, and which sometimes they will accept as a goal even when they know that it is an illusion. Love, fame, and religious certainty are all illusions of this sort: even at this date, then, *mysticisme* of certain kinds is seen as a *chimère*.

In *Voyage en Orient* Nerval quotes a passage from Fontenelle's *Histoire des Oracles*; if he knew Fontenelle's *Nouveaux Dialogues des Morts*,[30] he would have been especially interested in the imaginary dialogue between Raimond Lulle and Artémise. The name of this queen is one of the probable connotations of the title of 'Artémis', and the name of her husband ('Mausole') appears on a manuscript version of 'El Desdichado'; Nerval certainly knew her story, for he describes Catherine de Médicis as 'belle comme Vénus, et fidèle comme Arthémise' ('Quintus Aucler'; II, 1187). Fontenelle's dialogue is subtitled 'Sur la perfection où les Hommes aspirent', and it discusses the value to human beings of a *chimère*, which offers a stimulus to action; Raimond Lulle takes as an example the legendary devotion of Artémise to the memory of her dead husband:

Toutes les Sciences ont leur chimère après laquelle elles courent, sans la pouvoir attraper; mais elles attrapent en chemin d'autres connaissances fort utiles . . . la Morale a aussi sa chimère; c'est le désintéressement, la parfaite amitié. On n'y parviendra jamais, mais il est bon qu'on prétende y parvenir . . . Il faut qu'en toutes choses les hommes se proposent un point de perfection au-delà même de leur portée. Ils ne se mettraient jamais en chemin, s'ils croyaient arriver où ils arriveront effectivement . . . Qui vous eût dit que l'extrême fidélité dont vous vous piquiez, à l'égard de votre mari, n'était point naturelle, vous n'eussiez pas pris la peine d'honorer la mémoire de Mausole, par un Tombeau magnifique . . . Si par malheur la vérité se montrait telle qu'elle est, tout serait perdu . . .

The conscious and lucid acceptance of what he knew to be a *chimère*, an illusion, is constant in Nerval. The central episode of *Octavie* tells how the poet met in Naples a strangely fascinating girl, with whom he agreed to spend the night chiefly, it seems, because she reminded him of the woman he loved. The experience, which brought him more pain than pleasure, finds its way into 'Myrtho' as well as *Octavie*. An early version of the story, which obviously obsessed him for many years, was published in 1845 under the title 'L'Illusion'. He describes the girl in terms which echo his description of the nature of dreams: she is 'ce fantôme qui me séduisait et m'effrayait à la fois' (I, 289); and he seems always to have felt that love between man and woman depended on an illusion of this kind. Accepting the fact that the actress he worships from a distance already has a lover, he shrugs his shoulders at a friend's condolence: 'C'est une image que je poursuis, rien de plus' (*Sylvie*; I, 243). In 'Les Confidences de Nicolas' (which is more convincing as a self-portrait than as a study of Restif de la Bretone) Nerval makes Nicolas explain that what bewitched him in love was never the real woman he might have possessed, but 'une image que je me créais en moi-même . . . une chimère, fugitive comme un rêve, et que je ne songeais même pas à réaliser . . .' (II, 1071).

This constant rejection of reality in favour of the impossible ideal is attributed by Nerval himself to the atmosphere of disillusion and spiritual uncertainty in which his generation grew up. Their inheritance was one of defeat: military defeat at Waterloo in 1815; political defeat in Vienna, where the Congress which settled the future of Europe after the Napoleonic wars effectively reduced France to a subordinate rôle; perhaps even worse than all this, the destruction of the ideals of liberty, equality and fraternity which the Revolution had exalted and which events had proved to be hollow. There was a consequent loss of faith in secular government and the power of reason. The Orléans monarchy established in 1830 rejected the theory of Divine Right which the Bourbon Louis XVIII had tried to perpetuate; but its appeal to 'pure reason' proved no more popular in France. The evident materialism of this appeal encouraged a certain nostalgia, especially in the young, for the glories of the Napoleonic dream. At the same time the authority of priest and Church had been irrevocably damaged by the onslaughts of eighteenth-century *philosophie*, so that in the society of Louis-Philippe's time there was no ready-made alternative to materialistic reason. The possible attitudes in the face of such chaos were many and various, and could exist side by side in the same individual: they ranged from anger, revolt and despair to a calculated rejection of society; or in more sanguine temperaments, to aspirations towards some kind of spiritual salvation, through love of woman, love of art, socialist and spiritualist utopias, and esoteric religions of many different kinds. Nerval was astonishingly aware of the underlying causes, and of the inevitable results, of his own attitudes (*Sylvie*; I, 242):

Nous vivions alors dans une époque étrange, comme celles qui d'ordinaire succèdent aux révolutions ou aux abaissements des grands règnes ... c'était un mélange d'activité, d'hésitation et de paresse, d'utopies brillantes, d'aspirations philosophiques ou religieuses, d'enthousiasmes vagues, mêlés de certains instincts de renaissance; d'ennui des discordes passées, d'espoirs incertains ... L'ambition n'était cependant pas de notre âge, et l'avide curée qui se faisait alors des positions et des honneurs nous éloignait des sphères d'activité possibles. Il ne nous restait pour asile que cette tour d'ivoire des poètes, où nous montions toujours plus haut pour nous isoler de la foule. A ces points élevés ... nous respirions enfin l'air pur des solitudes, nous buvions l'oubli dans la coupe d'or des légendes, nous étions ivres de poésie et d'amour. Amour, hélas! des formes vagues, des teintes roses et bleues, des fantômes métaphysiques!

This rootless state, half-cynical, half-aspiring, is described in similar terms by Musset in the second chapter of *La Confession d'un Enfant du Siècle* (1836); he calls it 'la maladie du siècle'. In *Aurélia* (I, 385–6; this passage is discussed below), Nerval accurately traces it to its source in the destruction of religious belief, as Musset does in 'Rolla'.[31] Nerval is aware of a temptation to 'tomber dans l'excès contraire et d'essayer de se reprendre aux illusions du passé' (*Isis*; I, 300). Reason, however, was not so easily silenced, and being unable, like many men before and since, to reconcile the claims of heart and head, Nerval chose human love rather than divine love as his first instinctive reply to the uncertainties of his times. It is obvious that since it was primarily a substitute for vanished beliefs, this 'amour ... des fantômes métaphysiques' would be incapable of full realisation in a real woman: 'Vue de près, la femme réelle révoltait notre ingénuïté; il fallait qu'elle apparût reine ou déesse, et surtout n'en pas approcher' (*Sylvie*; I, 242). Moreover, it was more than likely that the disappointed seeker of the absolute would end by reviling what he had substituted for God. Nerval was lucidly aware of this danger:[32]

Vous vous êtes fait un dieu de tout excepté de Dieu. Vous avez élevé de faibles créatures, de faibles créations à la place, et ces créatures se sont brisées, rayées du monde. Vous vous êtes fait un dieu du Peuple, de la

Liberté. Et vous avez tremblé à le voir de près. Un dieu de l'amour, de l'amitié. Et quand ces divinités mensongères et fragiles ont été brisées par vous, vous avez nié.

One of the crimes of which Nerval accuses himself in *Aurélia* is an illusion of this kind: 'j'ai préféré la créature au créateur' (I, 389); eventually, it seems to him to be a kind of blasphemy.

Being only the reflection of the poet's frustrated desire for transcendence, woman inevitably appeared to have a sinister power, to be as much devil as goddess: 'La femme est la chimère de l'homme, ou son démon, comme vous voudrez, —un monstre adorable, mais un monstre . . .', he wrote in his introduction to Heine's *Intermezzo*, and described the pain in Heine's poems as 'la souffrance de l'âme aimant le corps, d'un esprit vivant lié à un charmant cadavre' (O.C. I, 89). Real woman was cold and unresponsive, a *chimère* like those that adorn the palace of Schönbrunn in *La Pandora* (I, 347–8): 'les chimères du vieux palais m'ont ravi mon cœur pendant que j'admirais leurs yeux divins et que j'espérais m'allaiter à leurs seins de marbre éclatant'. Jean Richer points to Rousseau as a possible source for the title of Nerval's sonnets,[33] and it seems certain that he would have known the celebrated passage from the *Confessions* (Book IX): 'L'impossibilité d'atteindre aux êtres réels me jeta dans le pays des chimères; et ne voyant rien d'existant qui fût digne de mon délire, je le nourris dans un monde idéal, que mon imagination créatrice eut bientôt peuplé d'êtres selon mon cœur'. There is, however, an essential difference: Nerval was aware, even as he pursued his ideal, of the dangers inherent in such an attachment to the impossible; thus every *chimère* was, like dream, 'attrayante et redoutable'. At the very end of *Sylvie*, which tells the story of the poet's attachment to just such a *chimère*, Nerval recognizes that the inevitable disillusionment brought by time is a kind of release (I, 271–3): 'Telles sont les chimères qui charment et égarent au matin de la vie . . . Les illusions tombent l'une après l'autre, comme les écorces d'un fruit, et le fruit, c'est l'expérience. Sa saveur est amère; elle a pourtant quelque chose d'âcre qui fortifie . . .' Nevertheless, Nerval did not regret having given himself up to the illusions 'qui charment et égarent', and the sight of Sylvie with her husband and children evokes only an

ambiguous sigh: 'Là était le bonheur peut-être . . . Cependant . . .'
He knew that the love that he imagined was not capable of con-
summation in this world. He conceived it as a thing of almost
impossible purity, strong and unchanging, sanctified by its
unique devotion to a single object. The *Lettres à Jenny Colon* bear
witness to the intensity of his desire for an ideal love, absolute and
eternal: 'Je vous aime autrement que les autres, moi': 'vous
n'êtes pas pour moi ce que sont les autres femmes'; 'Vous êtes la
première femme que j'aime et je suis peut-être le premier homme
qui vous aime à ce point. Si ce n'est pas là une sorte d'hymen que
le ciel bénisse, le mot amour n'est qu'un vain mot!'; 'mon amour
pour vous est ma religion' (I, 751, 758, 760). The theme recurs in
a manuscript note: 'Elle ne te choisira qu'à condition que tu sois
celui qui l'aurait aimée le plus, car les mariages sont marqués au
ciel' (I, 421). The idea of a unique and exclusive love is to be
found in *Les Chimères* also, in 'Antéros': 'protégeant tout seul ma
mère Amalécyte'; and in 'Artémis': 'celle que j'aimai seul m'aime
encor tendrement'. Love earned the consecration he dreamed of
by its absolute character, and by its refusal to accept compromises
or half-measures. Nor was it easily achieved: it demanded un-
remitting effort and the total sacrifice of self to the ideal. Though
he knew that such a dream, like the fidelity of Arthémise, was a
dream only ('les temps sont bien changés et les femmes aussi!'),
the *chimère* of perfect love was a necessary condition of his exis-
tence.

The other kind of *chimère* with which Nerval is concerned in his
sequence of sonnets is related to his experience of religion. Love
and religion are not really separate, however. When Nerval
grouped three of the eight poems of *Les Chimères* in *Petits Châteaux
de Bohême*, he linked them, despite their title *Mysticisme*, with the
story of a lost love:[34] 'Ma Cydalise, à moi, perdue, à jamais
perdue! . . . Une longue histoire, qui s'est dénouée dans un pays
du nord, —et qui ressemble à tant d'autres. Je ne veux ici que
donner le motif des vers suivants, conçus dans la fièvre et dans
l'insomnie. Cela commence par le désespoir et cela finit par la
résignation' (I, 75). The alternative to rebellious despair, it should
be noted, is not hope or certainty, but resignation; that is,
acceptance of what caused the despair. Throughout *Les Chimères*,
this movement from revolt to acceptance can be seen in the poet's

. .

attitude both to woman and to God. Love and religion often go hand in hand; in Romantic poetry in particular there is a tendency to replace the austerities of religious belief with a blend of eroticism and religiosity, such as one finds, for instance, in Chateaubriand's *Atala* or in Lamartine's poem 'Le Crucifix'. Nerval is entirely free from this tendency. Indeed he shows no eroticism at all, though he could be frankly sensual (and seems also to have been well acquainted with eighteenth-century erotic literature). If he links love with religion, it is because for him they were one and the same. Religion for Nerval was not an abstract *système*; it meant simply love of God. Thus whether he denies God or rejects woman, his essential problem is the difficulty of loving. It was not a problem conceived in abstract terms: Nerval's experience of love, and of its failure, within his own family, colours both his image of woman and his image of the Deity with whom he has such a troubled relationship. Lacking a mother, and subject for many years to the will of an unsympathetic father, he was led to turn away from the idea of a powerful God-the-Father, and seek religious comfort in the idea of a Goddess-mother; and that search further complicated his situation, since by idealizing woman he lessened his chances of finding what he needed in human love.

The *chimère* of religious certainty was made to seem remote for Nerval not only by his father's coldness, but also by the effects of his exposure in youth to the ideas of eighteenth-century *philosophie*, which made him unwilling to accept the authority of the Church against the evidence of reason (*Aurélia*; I, 393):

Je ne sais quelle fausse honte m'empêcha de me présenter au confessionnal; la crainte peut-être de m'engager dans les dogmes et dans les pratiques d'une religion redoutable, contre certains points de laquelle j'avais conservé des préjugés philosophiques. Mes premières années ont été trop imprégnées des idées issues de la Révolution, mon éducation a été trop libre, ma vie trop errante, pour que j'accepte facilement un joug qui sur bien des points offenserait encore ma raison. Je frémis en songeant quel chrétien je ferais si certains principes empruntés au libre examen des deux derniers siècles, si l'étude encore des diverses religions ne m'arrêtaient sur cette pente.

In *Aurélia* he charts the slow and painful progress of his attempts to reconcile his conflicting impulses; for he was, of course, pulled in two directions, by the claims of reason on the one hand, and by the need for belief on the other. This is the conflict he describes in the passage from *Sylvie* (I, 242) quoted above. Though reason would not be denied, reason alone was not enough: 'Philosophie! ta lumière, comme celle des enfers de Milton, ne sert qu'à rendre les ténèbres visibles' ('Paradoxe et Vérité'; I, 431). Worse, reason could poison the sources of spontaneous feeling, and weaken a man's faith in his own capacity to love; all emotional experience becomes material for 'la pensée d'un moraliste blasé', who turns it into 'une série d'observations physiologiques'; and the poet exclaims bitterly: 'qu'importe après tout? . . . nous ne vivons pas, nous n'aimons pas. Nous étudions la vie, nous analysons l'amour, nous sommes des philosophes, pardieu!' (*Voyage en Orient*; II, 61). In *Aurélia* his anguished conscience sees with remarkable clarity the issues involved; and incidentally makes clear the source of these difficulties in a conflict between father and son (I, 385–6):

Lorsque l'âme flotte incertaine entre la vie et le rêve, entre le désordre de l'esprit et le retour de la froide réflexion, c'est dans la pensée religieuse que l'on doit chercher des secours; —je n'en ai jamais pu trouver dans cette philosophie, qui ne nous présente que des maximes d'égoïsme ou tout au plus de réciprocité, une expérience vaine, des doutes amers . . . Mais pour nous, nés dans des jours de révolutions et d'orages, où toutes les croyances ont été brisées . . . —il est bien difficile, dès que nous en sentons le besoin, de reconstruire l'édifice mystique dont les innocents et les simples admettent dans leurs cœurs la figure toute tracée . . . L'ignorance ne s'apprend pas . . . Il ne faut pas faire si bon marché de la raison humaine, que de croire qu'elle gagne quelque chose à s'humilier tout entière, car se serait accuser sa céleste origine . . . Dieu appréciera la pureté des intentions sans doute, et quel est le père qui se complairait à voir son fils abdiquer devant lui tout raisonnement et toute fierté!

His own temerity immediately shocks him ('Ce sont des blasphèmes'), for if he was uneasy in the rôle of obedient Christian he was equally uneasy as a 'fils de Voltaire'; but most uneasy of all at the idea that there might be no God. Both 'Vers Dorés' and 'Le Christ aux Oliviers' spring from this dilemma, and concern themselves directly with it; while 'Horus' and 'Antéros', and, at a distance, 'Myrtho' and 'Artémis', refer more or less obliquely to the poet's personal difficulties in his relationship with his own father and in accepting the idea of a dominant deity.

The eternal struggle of man against the deity was symbolised by the Ancient Greeks in the myth of Prometheus. The rebellious Titan, half-god, half-man, is apparently absent from *Les Chimères*. But Nerval did not always offer his readers all the clues to his secrets. He does not mention Vergil's *Æneid* among the books whose inspiration lies close to the making of *Aurélia*, but contents himself with an oblique reference to the gates of ivory and horn (*Æneid* vi; 893–6); the spiritual quest of Aeneas was too close to Nerval's heart to be quoted as a literary parallel. In the same way, though the spirit of Prometheus pervades *Les Chimères*, his name is not mentioned in any of the sonnets. Yet he is the archetypal figure in the series Nerval offers us in 'Le Christ aux Oliviers': Icarus, Phaeton, Christ, and their darker brother Lucifer, who appears again in 'Antéros' as Anteros and Cain. The fire which the poet desires in 'Myrtho' is the fire which Prometheus stole from the gods, bringing upon himself eternal punishment.[35] Prometheus himself is hidden from our sight, except in a work which Nerval kept from publication even longer than *Les Chimères*, and whose eventual appearance in Dumas's *Le Mousquetaire* (31 October 1854) he bitterly regretted: *La Pandora*. According to the Greek myth, Pandora was fashioned from clay by the fire-god Hephaestus to tempt Prometheus's brother, Epimetheus, in retaliation for the theft of fire from heaven. At the end of his story, Nerval tells how he met 'l'artificieuse Pandora' a year after she had humiliated him (I, 356). He calls her 'enchanteresse', as he does Myrtho, and he is 'nailed' to the earth, as Prometheus was to his rock, by her smile, which is divine, as Myrtho was: 'un sourire divin me cloua sans forces sur le sol. "Te voilà encore, enchanteresse, m'écriai-je, et la boîte fatale, qu'en as-tu fait?"'. She tries to tempt him back, but he runs away:

... je me pris à fuir à toutes jambes ... «O fils des dieux, père des hommes! criait-elle, arrête un peu ... Où as-tu caché le feu du ciel que tu dérobas à Jupiter?»

Je ne voulus pas répondre: le nom de Prométhée me déplaît toujours singulièrement, car je sens encore à mon flanc le bec éternel du vautour dont Alcide m'a délivré.

O Jupiter! quand finira mon supplice?

Nerval recognised Prometheus for what he was originally intended to symbolise, and did not regard him merely as a poetic image of human suffering. This is made clear by his comments on Aeschylus's *Prometheus Unbound*,[36] in which he explicitly links Prometheus with the nineteenth-century Romantic hero:

'Ce qu'il est impossible de ne pas voir dans Prométhée, dit l'auteur, c'est une noble et magnifique personnification de la liberté humaine en lutte avec une puissance supérieure, de la pensée opprimée et non vaincue. Ce qui frappera tous les esprits, tous les cœurs, c'est cette profonde et généreuse compassion pour les misères de l'humanité, cette foi vive et sympathique en ses progrès, en ses destinées glorieuses et libres . . .' Il est certain qu'entre toutes ces pièces du théâtre grec fondées sur des traditions locales, parquées, pour ainsi dire, dans les limites d'une étroite fatalité, le *Prométhée délivré* ouvre seul à l'esprit des horizons infinis. Il brise du front ce ciel de saphir qui pèse sur le monde antique, et appelle à grands cris les dieux inconnus. Le poète qui osait en pleine Grèce et en plein paganisme nier l'éternité de Jupiter et annoncer la venue d'un révélateur nouveau, est certainement le père de toute cette famille de poètes sceptiques à qui nous devons aujourd'hui *Hamlet*, *Faust* et *Manfred*.

It is easy to recognise in this passage the themes of 'Le Christ aux Oliviers' and of 'Delfica'. Prometheus was punished for daring to measure himself against the deity: 'Il brise du front ce ciel de saphir . . .', like Nerval's own Christ, who cries 'J'ai touché de mon front à la voûte éternelle . . .' There are obvious references to sexual potency in *La Pandora*, as there are in 'Myrtho', but it is impossible to regard the image of fire as having only a sexual significance for Nerval.[37] It must be seen in the whole context of the poet's activity, and as the poet tells Pandora, we must take love and religion with equal seriousness, 'car c'est la même chose en vérité' (I, 349). The real pain of Prometheus's revolt derives from the fact that like Antéros, he would rather not have to rebel at all, he would prefer to love. Maud Bodkin points out that the true sense of the myth lies in the final reconciliation between Prometheus and Jupiter; Prometheus is not a symbol of rebellion, but of 'uttermost love, patient endurance, and forgiving pity'.[38] He begins as a Cain-like figure, and Fabre d'Olivet saw him thus:[39] 'On dirait . . . Caïn voguant avec Lucifer dans les abîmes du néant et de l'infini, sur les ailes poétiques de Lord Byron'. Musset, in 'Rolla', calls him 'Frère aîné de Satan'; and

Nerval compares Dante's Lucifer to the ancient Titan who fought against Jupiter (*Le Diable rouge*; II, 1218). But Prometheus ends as a figure like Christ. The tyrant can finally only be overthrown 'through love and insight ripening in the hero-victim's heart',[40] that is through understanding, acceptance and reconciliation, that 'résignation' of which Nerval speaks in *Petits Châteaux de Bohême* and which is a victory over the self rather than over any outside agency.

It is reconciliation that the poet has in view throughout *Les Chimères*. What he seeks is the perfection of love, in which the self is entirely given up. It represents for him a victory of a more profound, more lasting and more satisfying kind than the simple victories of self-assertion. But it remains a vision: none of the sonnets of *Les Chimères* expresses the fullness of victory achieved, though 'El Desdichado' comes near to it, with a victory of its own. Like *Aurélia*, these sonnets record the stages of the struggle. The final achievement of reconciliation gives to *Memorabilia*, the lyrical passages with which *Aurélia* nears its end, a unique and moving splendour; the *Chimères* can give us, for the most part, only a glimpse of imagined light.

The struggle which is recorded in *Les Chimères* was greatly complicated for Nerval by the kind of mental disturbance to which he was subject. His alternating moods of depression and elation caused him inevitably to see two alternating and quite different worlds, one bright and one dark. This was so throughout his life, and the pattern is only intensified, but not altered, by his periodic mental crises. His dual vision explains why the images in his poems are ranged in two apparently opposed groups, which are really contrasting aspects of the same things, so that every element of his experience appears in two guises, the fire-god both splendid and cruel, and woman both goddess and siren. For most of his life, Nerval was aware of this duality, and he was desperately concerned to make sense of it. His chief difficulty lay in the fact that he tended to see his dual nature in terms of good and evil, like those mediaeval thinkers who saw man aspiring to heaven and leaning towards the pit with equal desire. He is much concerned, when writing his Preface to Goethe's *Faust* (1840), with the passage in which Faust broods over his twin souls, 'dont l'une voudrait s'élancer après le soleil qui se retire,

et dont l'autre se débat encore dans les liens de la terre' (O.C.
I, 14). He could not help thinking in terms of a conflict (*Aurélia*;
I, 381):

Une idée terrible me vint: 'L'homme est double', me dis-je. —'Je sens
deux hommes en moi', a écrit un Père de l'Eglise. Le concours de deux
âmes a déposé ce germe mixte dans un corps qui lui-même offre à la vue
deux portions similaires reproduites dans tous les organes de sa structure.
Il y a en tout homme un spectateur et un acteur, celui qui parle et
celui qui répond. Les Orientaux ont vu là deux ennemis: le bon et le
mauvais génie. 'Suis-je le bon? suis-je le mauvais? me disais-je. En tout
cas, l'autre m'est hostile . . .'

Put in such terms, the question was of agonising urgency, for
while the good spirit might expect to be redeemed, the other was
doomed to eternal suffering. Nerval's preoccupation with this
problem is clearly reflected in *Les Chimères*, both as a question
about the poet's identity, and as a question about the universe as
a whole, whose destiny is one with his own. The problem of the
relative power of good and evil is already implicit in 'Le Christ
aux Oliviers' in 1844 (see commentary on this poem). Once he
became aware of the problem, it gathered urgency with every
mood of depression and doubt. The central revelation of *Aurélia*
comes at the point where the poet realises his oneness with the
natural world (I, 403), and feels the harmony which emanates
from every object he sees, and 'des couleurs, des odeurs et des
sons' (the phrase recalls his remark, quoted above, about Heine's
poems, in which love finds its rightful place 'au milieu des
formes, des couleurs et des sons'). But almost at once he saw that
the whole, of which he was an essential part, might be governed
not by good but by forces of evil (see commentary on 'Vers
Dorés'). The problem of '"Suis-je le bon? suis-je le mauvais? . . ."'
is now extended from the personal plane to include the whole of
creation. That he never managed to convince himself finally that
the universe was all good, is suggested by the fact that in 1854,
'Vers Dorés' stands at the end of the sequence of *Les Chimères*.
The circularity of Nerval's world meant that he could never
fully emerge from his dilemma. The beginning was also the
end, and the end another beginning: that is the lesson of
'Artémis'.

LANGUAGE AND FORM

The language and style of *Les Chimères* deserve close attention, for these poems are profoundly original and often extremely beautiful. The first thing to note is that they are sonnets, that is to say short poems of a rigid formal pattern. Within the scope of this pattern a certain play of internal rhyme and assonance and a certain flexibility of rhythm is possible, but the movement of the poem is always contained within a recognisable mould: indeed it is our constant awareness of that mould that gives meaning to the slight variations of form within it.

In the face of this formal control, it seems paradoxical to speak of incoherence; but the fact is that the poet can, if he wishes, agglomerate within the mould a number of quite unrelated ingredients. A 'nonsense' sonnet is, theoretically at least, perfectly possible. These sonnets, however, despite the fact that some critics have been tempted to call them incoherent, are not 'nonsense' sonnets. The formal coherence is not a disguise for mental confusion, but the expression of an inner unity. Every image, every word in *Les Chimères* is intimately linked with every other word and image. Their interaction is reinforced by the limited compass of the sonnet form, which enables the elements of the poem to make their effect on the reader almost simultaneously.

Within its fixed form the sonnet can show many variations; it can be rhetorical or conversational in tone, noble or colloquial in diction. Like any other fixed poetic form, it draws attention to the tradition to which it belongs, whether it imitates, adapts or largely rejects earlier models. Among Nerval's contemporaries, Lamartine, Vigny and Hugo preferred more accommodating forms; Sainte-Beuve on the other hand wrote many sonnets, and claimed to have achieved greater poetical intensity thereby: 'Tel filet d'idée poétique qui ... chez Lamartine s'épancherait en méditation et finirait par devenir fleuve ou lac, se congèle aussitôt chez moi, et se cristallise en sonnet ... Une idée dans un sonnet, c'est une goutte d'essence dans une larme de cristal'.[41] Sainte-Beuve was much influenced by English models: among those of his poems not in sonnet form, there are imitations of Kirke White, Collins, Gray, Southey and Coleridge; and his sonnets include translations or imitations of Lamb ('Le dernier des onze sonnets de Charles Lamb', in *Notes et Sonnets*), Keats ('Keen, fitful gusts', translated as 'Piquante est la bouffée', in *Poésies de Joseph Delorme*), Bowles and Wordsworth. But Sainte-Beuve's sonnets are generally discursive in the English Romantic manner, and they seem diffuse and slack beside Nerval's *Les Chimères*. There was no contemporary model for the kind of sonnet that Nerval writes, and he was looking back to the French sixteenth century, where his models were Ronsard, Du Bellay, and Du Bartas.

In 1830 Nerval published an anthology of the Pléiade poets. There was a renewed interest in the Renaissance at this time, and in 1827 the Académie had set as the subject for a prize essay, a study of the French poets of the sixteenth century. Nerval's entry did not win the prize, but he adapted his essay to form the basis of the introduction to his anthology.[42] In *Petits Châteaux de Bohême* (1853) he says of his early verses: 'en ce temps, je ronsardisais'. Nerval insists that he did not consciously imitate the sixteenth-century poets, but absorbed their manner naturally, as a result of his study of their work: 'étant admise l'étude assidue de ces vieux poètes, croyez bien que j'ai nullement cherché à en faire le pastiche, mais que leurs formes de style m'impressionnaient malgré moi, comme il est arrivé à beaucoup de poètes de notre temps' (I, 73). In his introduction, Nerval stresses the links between the Renaissance poets and the literature of classical antiquity, just as he remarks on the affinities with Greek culture which he saw in Goethe and in Heine, and says that Ronsard's *odelettes* were the models for his own *Odelettes*, in which indeed he makes use of the metres and rhythms of Ronsard and Du Bellay. There is still a great deal of the Pléiade in *Les Chimères*, but while Sainte-Beuve looks back to Du Bellay and Ronsard as his predecessors in the use of the sonnet,[43] Nerval seems to have been more influenced by the sonnets of Du Bartas. In one of the *Autres Chimères*, 'à Madame Sand' (I, 11), Nerval proclaims his kinship with Du Bartas:

> O seigneur Du Bartas! Je suis de ton lignage,
> Moi qui soude mon vers à ton vers d'autrefois ...

The first quatrain of 'à Madame Sand' is a quotation from the eighth sonnet of Du Bartas's *Les Neuf Muses Pyrénées*.

Sainte-Beuve, like many other critics, found Du Bartas's

style heavy and his language too often grotesquely inflated. Nevertheless, his two long poems, the *Première Sepmaine* or *Création du Monde* (which tells the story of the Creation) and the *Seconde Sepmaine* or *Enfance du Monde* (which recounts the expulsion from Eden and the murder of Abel) had a far-reaching influence, and besides his debt to the sonnets, Nerval may owe something to the boldness of Du Bartas's imagination in the longer poems. Du Bartas attempts to reconcile the religion he was born to and the classical culture he admired. This dual inheritance is one he shared with many writers of his own and of the following century: Milton's *Paradise Lost* owes much to Du Bartas, whose *Weekes* were widely read in England. Du Bartas claimed, not without reason, to be the only truly Christian poet of his time. It is a claim which Sainte-Beuve supported in his article on Du Bartas in 1842: 'Du Bartas, du premier jour, se posa comme un poète religieux. Ronsard et son école toute païenne régnait alors. Notre nouveau venu, au moins par le fond de l'inspiration, s'en détache . . .'.[44] The apparent contradiction between a Christian upbringing and a pagan tradition is dissolved in the grand sweep of Du Bartas's vision, as it is, at least temporarily, in *Les Chimères*. Nerval has not generally been regarded as a 'poète religieux'. It is a description for which, nonetheless, there is a great deal of justification.

In one respect the language of Du Bartas can also be seen to have influenced Nerval: the allegorical habit of the sixteenth-century poet's mind is present in *Les Chimères*, in which words are used in a way quite uncharacteristic of the nineteenth-century poets in general. When we read *Les Chimères*, we are aware of great areas of meaning pressing behind the printed words. The elements of the poet's imaginative world are defined by the words he uses, as the characters in an allegory are defined by their names. Moreover, the extent of the poet's world is precisely enclosed by the sonnet itself, each line of which constructs an aspect of that world. Henri Meschonnic has compared the force of many of Nerval's lines to that of *sentences*, maxims or proverbs with the air of eternal truths, sibylline or oracular in tone and in form, giving to each image the appearance of an enigmatic sign.[45] This effect is enhanced by the fact that the poet often simply juxtaposes his lines without explaining the connections between them:

> Mon front est rouge encor du baiser de la reine;
> J'ai rêvé dans la grotte où nage la syrène . . .

Thus placed, the verses catch and reflect each other's light, and seem to offer a meaning which lies not so much in the 'plain' sense of the individual images as in the complex structure to which they belong: that is, these images do not function separately, but all together. If A. J. Symons, Georges Rodenbach, Henri de Régnier and Rémy de Gourmont looked back to Nerval as an antecedent,[46] it is because words in Nerval's poems do seem to symbolise or evoke things rather than denote things; but they do so in a way quite different from the evocations of Symbolist poetry, and the Symbolists generally misunderstood Nerval's intentions. The word *évoquer* is the cause of the confusion. It would be more helpful to say that Nerval's words 'conjure up' the things he has in mind; they appear to us as extremely concrete objects, with an intense and mysterious inner life. But they are the creatures of Nerval's imagination, not of our own, and he defines them for us with an almost obsessive precision. He is not content, as the Symbolists in general are, to create a mood in which the reader can 'evoke' images of his own, and would never have said, as Valéry did later, 'Mes vers ont le sens qu'on leur prête'. Thus the 'fleur' to which Nerval refers more than once in *Les Chimères*, though its significance may change from one sonnet to the next, is never the flower which Mallarmé prefers, 'l'absente de tous bouquets'; it is not 'une fleur', but 'la *fleur* qui plaisait tant à mon cœur désolé' (the italics are Nerval's), a flower whose meaning is precisely defined by its place in the sonnet in which it stands.

The poet's aim in creating such images is not to set in motion a diffuse memory of our own, but to specify certain aspects of his experience, and especially to concentrate and crystallise that experience, as Nerval himself says many times: 'Il y a des années d'angoisse, de rêves, de projets qui voudraient se presser dans une phrase, dans un mot . . .' (*Lettres à Jenny Colon*; I, 766). Nerval attempts in his sonnets to imitate the power of time itself, but time as the human mind experiences it, 'qui concentre un siècle d'action dans une minute de rêve' (*Aurélia*, I, 368). Like Yousouf in *Voyage en Orient*, he achieves this by means of a language of heightened significance: 'il me venait des paroles d'une signification immense, des expressions qui renfermaient des univers de pensées, des phrases mystérieuses où vibrait l'écho des mondes disparus. Mon âme se grandissait dans le passé et dans l'avenir; l'amour que j'exprimais, j'avais la conviction de l'avoir ressenti de toute éternité' (II, 366). The poet is constantly striving to encompass and concentrate the formless mass of experience, and to express it in the fewest possible words: Nerval praises specifically, in Ronsard's *odelettes*, their 'forme concentrée' (I, 73), and admires Heine's gift for presenting 'des pensées de moraliste condensées en deux vers, en deux mots' (O.C. I, 87); he refers in the preface to *Les Filles du Feu* to the guiding principle of *Aurélia*: 'concentrer mes souvenirs' (I, 151). It is clear that each word in his sonnets will have to carry the greatest possible weight of meaning, and that each word will have to help to support and define the others. This is particularly true of the images in *Les Chimères*.

In the work of many poets, the image occupies a relatively unimportant place; it is often no more than, literally, an illustration, a sort of parable, a way of making more accessible to the reader a concept which might be difficult to grasp if expressed in abstract terms. This kind of image depends for its effect on being immediately recognisable and unequivocal, and it will therefore generally be drawn from a common stock of imagery. Similes are good examples of this kind of image: 'as dark as night', 'as cunning as the Devil'; of these two, one depends on common experience of the physical world, and the other on a common cultural background. Such images need not be simple in scope, though they frequently are. Rupert Brooke's image (in 'The Old Vicarage, Grantchester') of a river 'green as a dream and deep as death' uses elements of common experience, but creates with them quite complex and new associations, linking physical sensation with metaphysical idea.

An entirely different mechanism operates in the work of poets who use intensely personal images, relating to private associations of their own. Such images are endowed with a significance which may become clearer to the reader when he is sufficiently familiar with the writer's work. In some cases, however, he may never fully discover the associations of the images, and will then only be aware that they carry a charge of meaning undefined. A good poet will convince us that these mysterious images are important and perhaps precisely because they are mysterious. A mediocre poet will make us suspect that we are being tricked. There is a profound difference between *mystère* and *mystification*.

In the poetry of Nerval, the image occupies a privileged place. Most of his images are drawn from the common stock of European literature: names of places, names of gods, familiar elements of landscape, allusions to well-known legends and myths. Yet their mode of operation is peculiar to Nerval. If he mentions a legendary hero, or even so commonplace an object as a star or a flower, these things acquire a strongly personal significance through the context in which the poet has placed them: extract them from the words which accompany them in the sonnet, and they lose their identity. The effect of this is to create in the reader a sense that the poem is a world in itself, peopled by images which belong to that world and to no other. Certain images in Nerval's poems cannot wholly be explained even by reference to the same words in another of his works, for in another setting the same words may no longer be expressing the same concepts. An example of this is the celebrated 'soleil noir' of 'El Desdichado'. The image occurs also in Gautier's 'Melancholia'; and as Hélène Tuzet has pointed out,[47] in Dürer's engraving, to which Gautier explicitly refers, there is no black sun to be seen, but only a comet. Nerval himself refers, in the *Voyage en Orient*, to 'Le soleil noir de la mélancolie, qui verse des rayons obscurs sur le front de l'ange rêveur d'Albert Dürer' (II, 136). The image is also to be found in a poem by Heine, which Nerval translated, and which finds its way into 'Myrtho'. But whether or not Nerval believed that Dürer had drawn a black sun is not very important. What matters is that the image seemed to him to express perfectly the reversal of ordinary values which a state of acute depression induces, a reversal which he had personally experienced. That is clearly what the image expresses in *Voyage en Orient* (see commentary on 'El Desdichado'); but it bears only a slight relation to the 'noir soleil' of Heine's poem, and refers only incidentally to Gautier's 'Melancholia'; while in 'El Desdichado' it has become intensified and enlarged to the point where it is scarcely the same image at all, since it symbolises not merely a change of values, but a change of identity and of destiny.

The absolute specificity which characterises Nerval's more obviously personal images should warn us, furthermore, to be careful when interpreting those images in his poems which seem to be common property. Precisely because we think that we already know what these words represent, we are likely to introduce into the poem elements which do not belong to it. For example, there is a reference to the story of Cain and Abel in 'Antéros'. If we hastily assume that the poet is saying 'I am sometimes a murderer like Cain, and sometimes an innocent victim like Abel', we are likely to mistake the tone, and therefore the intention, of the poem. The images must be related not only to the contexts in which they have been used before, by this poet or by other poets, but also, and more importantly, to the poem in which they now appear.

The essence of the poet's meaning lies not in the series of particular incidents or figures of which the sonnets speak, but precisely in the coherence which the sonnet creates between the various elements of his experience. He is trying to sum up and make sense of that experience, of his whole life indeed, and the sense only becomes tangible when he has succeeded in expressing it within the bounds of a strict poetic form. Outside those bounds, the poet is no longer in control: 'L'art a toujours besoin d'une forme absolue et précise, en dehors de laquelle tout est trouble et confusion' (1840 Preface to *Faust*; O.C. I, 13). When Nerval begs Alexandre Dumas, in the preface to *Les Filles du Feu*, 'concédez-moi du moins le mérite de l'expression', he is telling us where the value of his poetry is to be found. The 'expression' which the poet achieves is nothing less than a world rescued from the formless mass of chaos. 'La dernière folie qui me restera peut-être, ce sera de me croire poète', he said; and he meant the word *poète* to be taken in its original sense of 'creator'. A poet, for Nerval, is not a rhymer who gives elegant expression to things already known. His task is literally to create, to make something new, to embody in his poem something which did not exist before, because the poem did not exist before. In one of his notebooks we find a prayer ('Paradoxe et Vérité'; I, 429):[48]

Je ne demande pas à Dieu de rien changer aux événements, mais de me changer relativement aux choses; de me laisser le pouvoir de créer autour de moi un univers qui m'appartienne, de diriger mon rêve éternel au lieu de le subir.

'Créer . . . un univers': there is no thought here of submitting to the flow of experience, least of all to the confusions of his own mind. The Surrealists were mistaken in thinking that Nerval's technique resembled their own. Nerval emphasises the necessity of lucidity and control, the need to make a pattern of what seems random. 'J'aime à conduire ma vie comme un roman', he wrote (*Voyage en Orient*; II, 342). He did not mean, as is sometimes suggested, that he liked to romanticise his experience. The operative word is *conduire*: life must be given a shape and a sequence, the coherence which belongs to art much more often than it belongs to life. Nerval's letters show how acutely conscious he was, at every turn, of making choices, of constructing his life as he lived it, and how often he would look back over past events and try to make sense of them, especially when he was temporarily removed from the protection of his customary routine, when travelling for instance (Letter to his father, 1839; I, 827): 'dans un si grand isolement que celui qui existe *à l'étranger*, on est porté toujours à jeter sur sa vie un regard d'ensemble et à soulever de grandes réflexions à propos de tout'. Nerval's constant efforts to turn the events of his life into myth should not be interpreted as mere delusions of grandeur; his aim in doing so was to relate the events of his life to a pre-existing pattern, so that their underlying meaning should be illuminated by the meaning of the myth. Nor was he in the least arrogant about his struggles. 'Je me jugeais un héros vivant sous le regard des dieux', he wrote in *Aurélia* (I, 403), but the phrase is not a claim to greatness: the hero, with the eye of the gods judging him, is a man who lives with full awareness in the constant presence of danger, with the constant threat of failure, required at every step to conquer his fears and to follow his hopes. Nerval makes no confident assertions of his strength. The long exploration of the world which he attempts in *Aurélia* begins with an admission of fear: 'Je n'ai pu percer sans frémir ces portes d'ivoire ou de corne qui nous séparent du monde invisible' (I, 359). The 'gates of ivory and horn' are the gates of Hades, described by Homer and by Vergil, through which dreams and illusions pass from the Underworld to the light of the world above. There are many moments of fear in *Les Chimères*; and when Adoniram descends to the heart of the mountain of Kaf, his guide repeatedly exhorts him 'Sois sans crainte' (*Voyage en Orient*; II, 556, 567–8). Fear is largely the source of the poet's efforts to create a controlled pattern of existence: on the one hand, a fear of disorder, and on the other, a fear of being overwhelmed by an order more powerful than himself, which might be either good or evil. Both these fears are resolved by the creation of an order of his own: poetry, in which the clarity and precision which are natural to him can be deployed to charm the magic forces of the universe into some kind of controllable movement. He speaks of art as 'L'Art par où l'homme active et complète l'œuvre de la création. Il soumet et spiritualise la matière'.[49] In Nerval's view, art is the only means by which man can to some degree control his universe, for, as the sonnets repeatedly attempt to show, man is only one element of a vast and complex organism, and his only hope of salvation lies in accepting the fact that he must therefore be passive as well as active, moved as well as moving. That art can encompass the universe, as the universe encompasses man, is clearly implied in the word *soumet*: art gives man the power to direct the elements of his environment, if only temporarily, in the way that he wishes, to create a world of his own with the materials the universe offers him. The word *spiritualise* seems further to suggest that in creating his new order, the poet or artist gives new meaning and value to the raw material of what he would otherwise apprehend as orderless things. He becomes himself a kind of god, compensating, by means of the order he has created, for his ignorance of the greater order which encompasses him: greater, that is, in physical size, but not in significance; for the microcosm of the sonnet reflects the face of the whole universe, both man and nature, and the poet, too, is a 'maker'. That is why when Nerval asked for the power to 'diriger mon rêve éternel au lieu de le subir', he added 'Alors, il est vrai, je serais Dieu'.

Les Chimères

El Desdichado

Je suis le ténébreux,—le veuf,—l'inconsolé,
Le prince d'Aquitaine à la tour abolie:
Ma seule *étoile* est morte,—et mon luth constellé
Porte le *Soleil noir* de la *Mélancolie*.   4

Dans la nuit du tombeau, toi qui m'as consolé,
Rends-moi le Pausilippe et la mer d'Italie,
La *fleur* qui plaisait tant à mon cœur désolé,
Et la treille où le pampre à la rose s'allie.   8

Suis-je Amour ou Phébus?... Lusignan ou Biron?
Mon front est rouge encor du baiser de la reine;
J'ai rêvé dans la grotte où nage la syrène...

Et j'ai deux fois vainqueur traversé l'Achéron: 12
Modulant tour à tour sur la lyre d'Orphée
Les soupirs de la sainte et les cris de la fée.

Myrtho

Je pense à toi, Myrtho, divine enchanteresse,
Au Pausilippe altier, de mille feux brillant,
A ton front inondé des clartés d'Orient,
Aux raisins noirs mêlés avec l'or de ta tresse.   4

C'est dans ta coupe aussi que j'avais bu l'ivresse,
Et dans l'éclair furtif de ton œil souriant,
Quand aux pieds d'Iacchus on me voyait priant,
Car la Muse m'a fait l'un des fils de la Grèce.   8

Je sais pourquoi là-bas le volcan s'est rouvert . . .
C'est qu'hier tu l'avais touché d'un pied agile,
Et de cendres soudain l'horizon s'est couvert.

Depuis qu'un duc normand brisa tes dieux d'argile,   12
Toujours, sous les rameaux du laurier de Virgile,
Le pâle Hortensia s'unit au Myrthe vert!

Horus

Le dieu Kneph en tremblant ébranlait l'univers:
Isis, la mère, alors se leva sur sa couche,
Fit un geste de haine à son époux farouche,
Et l'ardeur d'autrefois brilla dans ses yeux verts.　　4

«Le voyez-vous, dit-elle, il meurt, ce vieux pervers,
Tous les frimas du monde ont passé par sa bouche,
Attachez son pied tors, éteignez son œil louche,
C'est le dieu des volcans et le roi des hivers!　　8

L'aigle a déjà passé, l'esprit nouveau m'appelle,
J'ai revêtu pour lui la robe de Cybèle . . .
C'est l'enfant bien-aimé d'Hermès et d'Osiris!»

La Déesse avait fui sur sa conque dorée,　　12
La mer nous renvoyait son image adorée,
Et les cieux rayonnaient sous l'écharpe d'Iris.

Antéros

Tu demandes pourquoi j'ai tant de rage au cœur
Et sur un col flexible une tête indomptée;
C'est que je suis issu de la race d'Antée,
Je retourne les dards contre le dieu vainqueur.   4

Oui, je suis de ceux-là qu'inspire le Vengeur,
Il m'a marqué le front de sa lèvre irritée,
Sous la pâleur d'Abel, hélas! ensanglantée,
J'ai parfois de Caïn l'implacable rougeur!   8

Jéhovah! le dernier, vaincu par ton génie,
Qui, du fond des enfers, criait: «O tyrannie!»
C'est mon aïeul Bélus ou mon père Dagon...

Ils m'ont plongé trois fois dans les eaux du Cocyte,   12
Et protégeant tout seul ma mère Amalécyte,
Je ressème à ses pieds les dents du vieux dragon.

Delfica

La connais-tu, DAFNÉ, cette ancienne romance,
Au pied du sycomore, ou sous les lauriers blancs,
Sous l'olivier, le myrthe ou les saules tremblants,
Cette chanson d'amour . . . qui toujours recommence! 4

Reconnais-tu le TEMPLE, au péristyle immense,
Et les citrons amers où s'imprimaient tes dents?
Et la grotte, fatale aux hôtes imprudents,
Où du dragon vaincu dort l'antique semence. 8

Ils reviendront ces dieux que tu pleures toujours!
Le temps va ramener l'ordre des anciens jours;
La terre a tressailli d'un souffle prophétique . . .

Cependant la sibylle au visage latin 12
Est endormie encor sous l'arc de Constantin:
—Et rien n'a dérangé le sévère portique.

Artémis

La Treizième revient . . . C'est encor la première;
Et c'est toujours la seule,—ou c'est le seul moment:
Car es-tu reine, ô toi! la première ou dernière?
Es-tu roi, toi le seul ou le dernier amant? . . .   4

Aimez qui vous aima du berceau dans la bière;
Celle que j'aimai seul m'aime encor tendrement:
C'est la mort—ou la morte . . . O délice! ô tourment!
La rose qu'elle tient, c'est la *Rose trémière*.   8

Sainte napolitaine aux mains pleines de feux,
Rose au cœur violet, fleur de sainte Gudule:
As-tu trouvé ta croix dans le désert des cieux?

Roses blanches, tombez! vous insultez nos dieux: 12
Tombez fantômes blancs de votre ciel qui brûle:
—La sainte de l'abîme est plus sainte à mes yeux!

Le Christ aux Oliviers

Dieu est mort! le ciel est vide . . .
Pleurez! enfants, vous n'avez plus de père!
J E A N P A U L

I

Quand le Seigneur, levant au ciel ses maigres bras,
Sous les arbres sacrés, comme font les poëtes,
Se fut longtemps perdu dans ses douleurs muettes,
Et se jugea trahi par des amis ingrats;   4

Il se tourna vers ceux qui l'attendaient en bas
Rêvant d'être des rois, des sages, des prophètes . . .
Mais engourdis, perdus dans le sommeil des bêtes,
Et se prit à crier: «Non, Dieu n'existe pas!»   8

Ils dormaient. «Mes amis, savez-vous *la nouvelle*?
J'ai touché de mon front à la voûte éternelle;
Je suis sanglant, brisé, souffrant pour bien des jours!

Frères, je vous trompais: Abîme! abîme! abîme!   12
Le dieu manque à l'autel, où je suis la victime . . .
Dieu n'est pas! Dieu n'est plus!» Mais ils dormaient toujours!

II

Il reprit: «Tout est mort! J'ai parcouru les mondes;
Et j'ai perdu mon vol dans leurs chemins lactés,
Aussi loin que la vie, en ses veines fécondes,
Répand des sables d'or et des flots argentés: 4

Partout le sol désert côtoyé par des ondes,
Des tourbillons confus d'océans agités . . .
Un souffle vague émeut les sphères vagabondes,
Mais nul esprit n'existe en ces immensités.   8

En cherchant l'œil de Dieu, je n'ai vu qu'un orbite
Vaste, noir et sans fond; d'où la nuit qui l'habite
Rayonne sur le monde et s'épaissit toujours;

Un arc-en-ciel étrange entoure ce puits sombre,   12
Seuil de l'ancien chaos dont le néant est l'ombre,
Spirale, engloutissant les Mondes et les Jours!

III

«Immobile Destin, muette sentinelle,
Froide Nécessité!... Hasard qui t'avançant,
Parmi les mondes morts sous la neige éternelle,
Refroidis, par degrés l'univers pâlissant,   4

Sais-tu ce que tu fais, puissance originelle,
De tes soleils éteints, l'un l'autre se froissant...
Es-tu sûr de transmettre une haleine immortelle,
Entre un monde qui meurt et l'autre renaissant?...   8

O mon père! est-ce toi que je sens en moi-même?
As-tu pouvoir de vivre et de vaincre la mort?
Aurais-tu succombé sous un dernier effort

De cet ange des nuits que frappa l'anathème...   12
Car je me sens tout seul à pleurer et souffrir,
Hélas! et si je meurs, c'est que tout va mourir!»

IV

Nul n'entendait gémir l'éternelle victime,
Livrant au monde en vain tout son cœur épanché;
Mais prêt à défaillir et sans force penché,
Il appela le *seul*—éveillé dans Solyme: 4

«Judas! lui cria-t-il, tu sais ce qu'on m'estime,
Hâte-toi de me vendre, et finis ce marché:
Je suis souffrant, ami! sur la terre couché . . .
Viens! ô toi qui, du moins, as la force du crime!»   8

Mais Judas s'en allait mécontent et pensif,
Se trouvant mal payé, plein d'un remords si vif
Qu'il lisait ses noirceurs sur tous les murs écrites . . .

Enfin Pilate seul, qui veillait pour César,   12
Sentant quelque pitié, se tourna par hasard:
«Allez chercher ce fou!» dit-il aux satellites.

V

C'était bien lui, ce fou, cet insensé sublime . . .
Cet Icare oublié qui remontait les cieux,
Ce Phaéton perdu sous la foudre des dieux,
Ce bel Atys meurtri que Cybèle ranime!   4

L'augure interrogeait le flanc de la victime,
La terre s'enivrait de ce sang précieux . . .
L'univers étourdi penchait sur ses essieux,
Et l'Olympe un instant chancela vers l'abîme.   8

«Réponds! criait César à Jupiter Ammon,
Quel est ce nouveau dieu qu'on impose à la terre?
Et si ce n'est un dieu, c'est au moins un démon . . .»

Mais l'oracle invoqué pour jamais dut se taire;   12
Un seul pouvait au monde expliquer ce mystère:
—Celui qui donna l'âme aux enfants du limon.

Vers Dorés

Eh quoi! tout est sensible!
PYTHAGORE

Homme, libre penseur! te crois-tu seul pensant
Dans ce monde où la vie éclate en toute chose?
Des forces que tu tiens ta liberté dispose,
Mais de tous tes conseils l'univers est absent.   4

Respecte dans la bête un esprit agissant:
Chaque fleur est une âme à la Nature éclose;
Un mystère d'amour dans le métal repose;
«Tout est sensible!» Et tout sur ton être est puissant.   8

Crains, dans le mur aveugle, un regard qui t'épie:
A la matière même un verbe est attaché...
Ne la fais pas servir à quelque usage impie!

Souvent dans l'être obscur habite un Dieu caché;   12
Et comme un œil naissant couvert par ses paupières,
Un pur esprit s'accroît sous l'écorce des pierres!

COMMENTARIES

FOREWORD

The text of this edition is that printed in the volume *Les Filles du Feu* in 1854, the only edition known to have been revised by the poet himself.

A recent work by M. Jean Guillaume offers an exhaustive examination of the various known versions of each of the poems of *Les Chimères*, including manuscripts, publications in reviews, fragments in notes to the printers of *Les Filles du Feu*, and all related documents.[50] In view of this extremely thorough treatment of the text, I have not attempted, in the Introduction, Commentaries and Notes to the present volume, to reproduce all the relevant documents. Most of them are, in any case, of little help in understanding the poems themselves. M. Guillaume also discusses at length the problems of dating raised by the different versions. Some of his conclusions remain conjectural, and therefore disputable; I would not however wish to add to the controversy about the dating of *Les Chimères*, were it not that the text, as it appears in *Les Filles du Feu*, raises a problem that seems to have a real importance for our understanding of the poems: the order in which we read them.

When the sonnets appeared in 1854, they were arranged, presumably by Nerval himself, in an order which bears no discernible relation to the order in which those previously published had appeared. It might be thought that this is a trivial matter. Poets frequently arrange their poems within a volume in a sequence whose principle is not clear to anyone else, and which may be dictated by nothing more than a desire to produce a suitable variety of tone. There are grounds for regarding arrangement of any kind as a pointless exercise, since a poet has no way at all of ensuring that the reader will actually read his poems in the order which he himself would prefer; but the fact remains that he will often try to indicate that the order is important. Not only will our reading of a poem be affected by the poem we read before it, but the second poem may affect our view of the first in retrospect; and both will then affect the following poem, and so on. A recently published collection of sonnets, Jacques Roubaud's ε, exploits this effect experimentally by offering the reader three alternative reading sequences, to be followed at different times, as well as the option of ignoring these suggestions and inventing an order of his own. The writer's purpose was 'to show that each poem, read by itself, assumes a different value when read in relationship to the poems surrounding it; and that each method of reading reveals a different aspect of the text'.[51]

We know that 'Le Christ aux Oliviers' was published in 1844, 'Vers Dorés' and 'Delfica' in 1845; and I have indicated the reasons for believing that 'Myrtho' and 'Horus' date from the same period, and 'Antéros' possibly from a somewhat later one. 'Artémis' is related to *L'Imagier de Harlem*, performed in 1851; while 'El Desdichado', which always accompanies 'Artémis' in the manuscripts, is impossible to date with any certainty, though it seems to be related to *Sylvie*, which Nerval wrote and published in 1853, and Dumas believed that 'El Desdichado' was written just before Nerval gave him the manuscript, in November 1853. Since the sequence of the poems in *Les Filles du Feu* is clearly not chronological ('El Desdichado' is placed first, and 'Vers Dorés' last), we must wonder why Nerval chose to arrange them as he did.

The order in which the sonnets were printed in 1854 leads one, following certain key words which are echoed from one sonnet to the next, to perceive a sequence of ideas which we might schematise as follows:

'El Desdichado':	Pausilippe / grotte / reine-syrène
'Myrtho':	Pausilippe / Muse-Grèce / volcan / dieux brisés
'Horus':	Dieu des volcans / geste de haine / mort d'un dieu / esprit nouveau
'Antéros':	Geste de haine / esprit nouveau (dents du dragon)
'Delfica':	Semence du dragon / retour des dieux (ils reviendront) = esprit nouveau
'Artémis':	Retour éternel (revient) / doute (es-tu reine? as-tu trouvé ta croix? désert des cieux) / la mort / geste de haine (vous insultez nos dieux)
'Le Christ aux Oliviers':	Désert des cieux / doute (as-tu pouvoir de vivre?)/ mort d'un dieu / renaissance-mystère
'Vers Dorés':	Mystère d'amour / la vie éclate en toute chose (renaissance)

It will be seen that there is some cross-reference within the pattern, but that it is possible to trace a kind of development from first to last, through the key words which appear to represent recurring attitudes. This sequence has a strange effect on the poems, for not only do they appear to follow logically upon those that precede them on the page, but they also influence our view of the poems they follow. For instance, when 'El Desdichado' appeared in 1853, its editor, Dumas, insinuated that the sonnet was a proof of Nerval's insanity, and it is no doubt partly to refute this suggestion that Nerval places 'El Desdichado' first, so that it acts as preface to the group. He gives us 'Myrtho' next; and the reference to the 'Pausilippe altier de mille feux brillant' in 'Myrtho', reflects the *mille feux* back on to 'El Desdichado'. We are inclined then to see 'El Desdichado' as a sonnet primarily concerned with a love scene set on Posilipo, as 'Myrtho' appears to be, to interpret 'toi qui m'as consolé' as referring to a woman who in 'Myrtho' is called 'divine enchanteresse', and to leave largely out of account those elements which seem unrelated to 'Myrtho'. Similarly, the effect of 'Artémis', which is intensely disturbing if we concentrate on this sonnet alone, is greatly diminished by the apparently hopeful tone of the ending of 'Le Christ aux Oliviers' which follows it, and seems altogether dispelled by 'Vers Dorés'.

The whole sequence, as it stands, appears to begin with a gentle melancholy and to end with a serene optimism. The 'désespoir', the 'fièvre', of which Nerval speaks in *Petits Châteaux de Bohême* are consequently obscured. We may attribute his action in arranging the sonnets in this order to his familiar diffidence, to which his friend Gautier bears witness:[52]

> Gérard de Nerval cherchait l'ombre avec le soin que mettaient les autres à chercher la lumière; nature choisie et délicate, talent fin et discret, il aimait à s'envelopper de mystère . . . [il] semblait prendre plaisir à s'absenter de lui-même, à disparaître de son œuvre, à dérouter le lecteur . . .

The poet was profoundly unwilling to call attention to himself, and in obeying a compulsion to speak, he has resisted the temptation to raise his voice. What he has to tell us is told for the most part obliquely; whenever he felt that he was about to recount anything that might allow his reader to guess at real acquaintances, real circumstances, real pain, he drew back: 'je me suis rappelé à temps le vers de Klopstock: "Ici la Discrétion me fait signe de son doigt d'airain" '.[53] He would not allow the public to see the raw material of his art, before the poet had shaped and ordered the experiences of the man. In 1843, just before the publication of the first of *Les Chimères*, and thinking no doubt of Vigny's poem 'La Mort du Loup' which had just been published, he wrote: 'J'ai la pudeur de la souffrance, comme l'animal blessé qui se retire dans la solitude pour y souffrir longtemps ou pour y succomber sans plainte' (*Voyage en Orient*; II, 93). An early fragment of dialogue mocks the Romantic manner:[54]

> . . . je ne me sens ni d'humeur, ni de complexion à m'en aller gravir les Alpes comme Obermann, parcourir les bois effeuillés . . . comme en étendant les bras et criant 'O nature!' Je sais qu'il y a encore la poésie intime comme la cendre du foyer, la contemplation d'un mur lézardé et moisi, les rêveries autour des tombeaux sous les peupliers mélancoliques. Analyser ses maux et les montrer avec orgueil.

The suffering in *Les Chimères* is deliberately veiled. If we are to appreciate the extent to which these poems are the record, and the examination, of a spiritual agony not less crucial than the Agony in the Garden described in 'Le Christ aux Oliviers', we ought to observe the poet's progress as nearly as possible as it actually happened: we ought to read the sonnets in the order in which they were written.[55] We cannot unfortunately know this order with any degree of accuracy, though we can be guided by the factors I have outlined above. A further guide may be found in the text of *Aurélia*, which was completed after the publication of *Les Filles du Feu*, and sets out to analyse the spiritual crises which are reflected in the sonnets. In *Aurélia*, faith in God and in immortality is finally achieved only after the poet has confronted the God he feared, and learned to love Him. The same sequence of events may be observed in *Les Chimères*; and I propose to follow that sequence in the Commentaries and Notes which follow. The reader is, of course, still at liberty to invent his own sequence, or to follow Nerval's: indeed, he should do so, for no one account of these poems can claim to be definitive, and whatever the reader can bring to them in the way of relevant understanding will help to illumine their mystery.

LE CHRIST AUX OLIVIERS

This five-part poem (p. 49) was the first of *Les Chimères* to be published. It appeared, with very minor variants, in *L'Artiste*, on 31 March 1844, that is about a year before the publication of 'Vers Dorés'. It is the only long poem in Nerval's mature work, and appears to be his only attempt at the long narrative poem which was popular with the early Romantic school. However, this is not true narrative poetry, since the story itself is of less importance than the issues it raises and the ideas it allows the poet to discuss. Moreover, although the narrative and discussion are extended, the form is not that of a long poem in the ordinary sense: 'Le Christ aux Oliviers' is a sequence of five sonnets, and each is self-contained to the extent that each deals fully with one aspect of the central theme. But each is carefully linked to the next, and the whole sequence encloses its theme in a circle, returning ultimately to its starting-point. The poem has thus as clearly defined a shape as the rest of the poems of *Les Chimères*.

In style these five sonnets are discursive, and rather less tightly knit than the other sonnets of *Les Chimères*. There is a clear narrative thread, and the descriptive passages are both lucid and relevant to the drama. All this makes the poem impressively vivid, but its form contributes less to the total effect than does the power of a few striking images: the wasted limbs of Christ, the dead suns revolving in the eternal snows of space, the discontent of Judas. The very few amendments which Nerval made to his original version certainly improve the sound of the poem: 'Mais nul esprit *n'habite* en ces immensités' becomes 'Mais nul esprit *n'existe* en ces immensités' (sonnet II, l. 8); 'Cet *Athys immolé* que Cybèle ranime' becomes 'Ce *bel Atys meurtri* que Cybèle ranime' (V, l. 4); and '*la céleste* victime' becomes '*l'éternelle* victime' (IV, l. 1); but harmony of sound is not the poet's only concern, for these alterations also reinforce the sense of the poem. Clarity and precision seem to have been an important consideration at this stage.

The subject of the poem is Christ's agony on the Mount of Olives. The first published version bears the sub-title 'Imitation de Jean-Paul'. At its second publication in *Petits Châteaux de Bohême* (1853), the sub-title is replaced by an epigraph:

> Dieu est mort! le ciel est vide . . .
> Pleurez! enfants, vous n'avez plus de père!

with the attribution JEAN PAUL. This epigraph is taken from Jean-Paul Richter's *Reden des toten Christus vom Weltgebaüde herab, dass kein Gott sei*, a curious text, more prose-poem than discourse, which was partially translated by Madame de Staël and published in her book *De l'Allemagne* in 1810. Nerval knew and quoted from Madame de Staël's book, but he himself translated other texts by Richter between 1830 and 1840, and must have also known the German original, since he borrows some expressions left untranslated by Madame de Staël. The ideas and images of Richter's *Dream*, as it is known, had an extraordinarily wide influence on the French Romantics (though Vigny's poem 'Le Mont de Oliviers' (1844) was probably inspired by another text by Richter). The image of the empty eye-socket radiating darkness, which Richter's Christ sees in his vision, can be found in Hugo's poems, and in one of his drawings; and it is one possible source for the *soleil noir* of Nerval's 'El Desdichado.[56]

However, while the theme was obviously attractive to many writers, the treatment of that theme depends on the individual writer's attitudes and intentions. The briefest comparison of Nerval's poem with Vigny's 'Le Mont de Oliviers', for instance, makes it clear that Nerval, like Vigny, develops the theme in accordance with preoccupations of his own, and the conclusions he comes to are those compatible with his own temperament, and quite different from Vigny's conclusions.

Like 'Vers Dorés', 'Le Christ aux Oliviers' appears to offer the reader few obscurities. Carried along by the familiar narrative, we may easily miss the essential preoccupation of the poem, and notice only the remarkable freshness with which the successive incidents are described. Like 'Horus' and 'Antéros', this poem uses direct speech to present the action in an intensely dramatic way. The characters are brought to life with the minimum of description: 'Pilate . . . sentant quelque pitié'; 'Judas s'en allait, mécontent et pensif, Se trouvant mal payé . . .'; 'Quand le Seigneur, levant au ciel ces maigres bras . . .' The economy of means is remarkable: in the very first line of the poem, the one word *maigres* carries a complete image of Christ's agony, where Vigny uses a relatively extended description to achieve the same effect.

But the familiar story, however vividly told, is by no means the dominant feature of the poem. Two of the five sonnets are entirely concerned with a description and attempted explanation of Christ's vision of the universe, and the final sonnet relates the figure of Christ to a conception of the universe which has found expression in many different symbols in the course of human history. The presence of this general theme affects, as one would expect, the way in which the narrative is presented.

I. The first sonnet (p. 49) poses the image of Christ as a completely human figure, quite unlike the 'figure rayonnante, noble, élevée' of Jean-Paul's *Dream*.[57] His humanity is not explicitly discussed, as it is in Vigny's 'Le Mont des Oliviers' or in Lamartine's 'Le Crucifix'; we are made to feel it in Christ's physical fragility, in his pain, and in the immediate analogy with poets, made both directly in 'comme font les poëtes' and indirectly in the reference to 'les arbres sacrés', reminding us that olive groves were once sacred to Apollo and the Muses. Perhaps there is also a reference, in the tenth line, to Horace's glorification of the poet (*Odes* I, i, 35–6): 'Quodsi me lyricis vatibus inseres, / sublimi feriam sidera vertice'; in Villeneuve's translation: 'si tu me donnes une place parmi les lyriques inspirés, j'irai, au haut des airs, toucher les astres de ma tête'. Christ's humanity gives added weight to the Biblical terms 'mes amis' and 'frères'; it is to human beings like himself that Christ brings '*la nouvelle*'. In *Aurélia*, the poet, convinced at last of the soul's immortality, comes like the angels bearing 'good tidings of great joy': 'C'est alors que je suis descendu parmi les hommes pour leur annoncer l'heureuse nouvelle' (I, 410). In this sonnet, the tidings which Christ has to offer are the cause of his suffering, which, though it is evoked for us in physical terms ('Je suis sanglant, brisé . . .'), is a moral suffering. He has discovered that there is no God, having confirmed the emptiness of the universe by ascending to the heights of heaven: 'J'ai touché de mon front à la voûte éternelle . . .' This idea is not further explored here, but it foreshadows the links, in the final sonnet of this poem, with Icarus and Phaeton:

> Cet Icare oublié qui remontait les cieux,
>
> Ce Phaéton perdu sous la foudre des dieux . . .

The juxtaposition of these verses parallels that of the two tercets in the first sonnet: the discovery, and its attendant suffering, seem to be a punishment for Christ's temerity in climbing to the *voûte éternelle*, as Icarus's fall was a punishment for daring to fly too near the sun, and Phaeton's for daring to drive the chariot of his father, the sun-god Apollo. Horace (*Odes* IV, xi, 25–31) cites Phaeton as an example of the sacrilege involved in placing one's hopes higher than a man may reach. It is dangerous, it seems, for men to measure themselves against the gods.

II. The second sonnet (p. 50) describes the universe that Christ has seen in his journey through space. The first quatrain evokes a rapturous free flight, through images of brilliance and plenitude; Jean-Paul's text is colourless in comparison: 'J'ai parcouru les mondes, je me suis élevé au-dessus des soleils, et là aussi il n'est point de Dieu . . .' Nerval's sonnet stresses at this point the beauty of the universe:

> J'ai parcouru les mondes;
> Et j'ai perdu mon vol dans leurs chemins lactés,
> Aussi loin que la vie, en ses veines fécondes,
> Répand des sables d'or et des flots argentés . . .

In the second quatrain the same images are dramatically converted into images of confusion; the golden sands become a shifting desert, the streams become agitated whirlpools:

> Partout le sol désert côtoyé par des ondes,
> Des tourbillons confus d'océans agités . . .

Without the *esprit* which should direct it, the universe becomes chaos again, and the planets wander aimlessly in space ('les sphères vagabondes').

The light with which, according to Genesis, God began the creation of order from chaos, is also converted into its opposite: where the eye of God, the sun, should be, there is only a bottomless well of darkness ('ce puits sombre'). Darkness here is not merely the absence of light. Jean-Paul's image of 'un orbite vide, noir et sans fond'[58] is an image of death, which is repeated in his description of a ghost: 'La place de l'œil était vide'. Nerval has added the notion of a positive and ever-deepening blackness which radiates from the central horror like the fires of hell in Milton's *Paradise Lost*: 'No light; but only darkness visible'.[59] In *Aurélia* Nerval tells us how, as a child, he was disturbed by images of the classical gods, finding them more awe-inspiring than the worn images of saints in the village church. 'Embarrassé au milieu de ces divers symboles, je demandai un jour à mon oncle ce que c'était que Dieu. "Dieu, c'est le soleil", me dit-il' (I, 394). In 'Le Christ aux Oliviers' that sun has become a source of darkness, from which the spirit of Christ recoils. The power of God appears to have been nullified; but it is not yet clear what has replaced it. The universe may be running backwards towards chaos, or it may have been conquered by the powers of darkness.

The well of night is also described as a whirlpool, in which time and space are swallowed up: 'Spirale, engloutissant les Mondes et les Jours . . .' The well and the whirlpool reappear in *Les Nuits d'Octobre* when Nerval speaks of Dante's Inferno: 'les cercles ténébreux dont la spirale immense se rétrécit toujours, pour aboutir à ce puits sombre où

Lucifer est enchaîné jusqu'au jour du dernier jugement' (I, 92). Above the darkness a rainbow curves.[60] The poet calls the rainbow *étrange*, and its presence here is certainly unexpected. To the Greeks it was the scarf of Iris, messenger of the gods, and in that guise it appears in 'Horus';[61] in the Old Testament account of the Flood, it is the sign of the renewal of God's pact with man, and the beginning of a new world. In his *Poésies allemandes* (1830),[62] Nerval gives his translation of a poem by Klopstock, 'Les Constellations', in which he describes the rainbow as a message from God: 'l'arc céleste, l'arc de grâce et de consolation que sa main tendit dans les nuages'. Again, in his description of Bouton's Diorama,[63] an interesting text which recalls certain passages in *Aurélia*, Nerval describes the rainbow which appears after the Flood as 'L'arc-en-ciel, signe du pardon céleste' (II, 1236). In 'Le Christ aux Oliviers', the rainbow seems intended as such a sign. Everything in the universe is dead, as far as the eye of Christ can see: 'Tout est mort!'; and the darkness he perceives is only the threshold of the ultimate, deeper darkness, 'l'ancien chaos', that which was before God called light into being, and to which, it seems, the universe is about to return. But the description in the second quatrain seems to have echoes of the Flood in it: 'le sol désert côtoyé par des ondes ... océans agités ...'; and the rainbow is a glimpse of a possible hope. Perhaps what appears to be dead may be restored to life?

III. The third sonnet (p. 51) begins by picking up the theme of undirected movement which occurs in the second sonnet, but the idea of absence of control is here replaced with something more positive. From 'nul esprit n'existe en ces immensités', we move to the notion of a controlling force of a kind: chance, whom the Romans called also Necessity or Destiny, a capricious, watchful deity with whom there can be no communication: 'muette sentinelle'.[64] In this first quatrain, the agitated universe of the second sonnet gradually runs down before our eyes, like a clockwork movement whose spring has uncoiled; and the whole machine, 'par degrés', is stilled (*immobile ... sentinelle ... morts*). The universe becomes colourless and cold, silent and shrouded in snow (*muette ... froide ... la neige éternelle ... refroidis ... pâlissant ... soleils éteints*). The image of the 'sphères vagabondes' is disturbing in a splendidly apocalyptic way; these 'soleils éteints, l'un l'autre se froissant' are infinitely more disturbing, chillingly evocative of the last spasms of a dying creature.

This vision of the cold stillness of death fills Christ with anguish, and he calls on the spirit whose eternal presence is now no longer denied ('puissance originelle'). But the nature of that power seems beyond apprehension, since its action appears as mere 'Hasard', and frightened by his vision of the dead suns, Christ questions whether the spirit is really acting according to a plan. Can it really take the life from a dying world and reincarnate it in one about to be born again?

> Es-tu sûr de transmettre une haleine immortelle
> Entre un monde qui meurt et l'autre renaissant?

The *renaissant* is important here, for it implies a continuous process, in which life passes endlessly through the various forms of matter, each waiting to be reborn when its time comes round again.[65]

But is it not equally likely that the living essence will be lost in limbo? Is reincarnation, or rebirth, possible at all? The first tercet shifts the scope of this question from the imagined universe to a more personal level, while the invocation *O mon père*! makes it plain that Christ has moved further still from the position of the first sonnet. We have been moving gradually towards this invocation from the beginning: in the first sonnet from *Dieu n'est pas* to *Dieu n'est plus*, implying that God did once exist; in the second sonnet from *nul esprit n'existe* to the opposed images of a positive darkness and a rainbow; in this third sonnet from the undefined *puissance originelle*, whose action seems mere chance, to *mon père*. Yet there is no certainty of God's existence, for the sonnet ends with questions whose answer we cannot know; and indeed they do not seem to expect an answer at all. They are rhetorical questions whose function in the poem is to express a fear: perhaps it is not God whose presence Christ feels, perhaps God has died like the suns which He created. At this point another possibility occurs to Christ: there may be an even more positive force than chance at work. Perhaps the 'ange des nuits' whom God defeated has overthrown his oppressor and now controls the universe. This power of darkness whose name was once Lucifer,[66] the 'bearer of light', recalls the positive darkness radiating from the 'orbite Vaste, noir et sans fond' of the second sonnet. Like Lucifer, the universe may have become a negative image of itself: the pattern appears the same, but light has become darkness, and good evil.

Of the alternatives which this sonnet offers, it is evident that 'hasard' excludes evil, and evil excludes 'hasard'; and Christ's dilemma is complete, for neither possibility is acceptable. Christ's fear that evil may have triumphed is linked, in the final lines of this sonnet, to his feeling that he is alone in his suffering. He cannot feel God within him; and this means not only that he is alone, but that his suffering has no meaning and no sanctifying purpose. This idea reflects the conception of a purposeless universe which we find in the second sonnet. If 'Vers Dorés' describes a universe in which a *pur esprit* gives value to all things, including man, 'Le Christ aux Oliviers' offers its counterpart: a universe turned to chaos by the absence of that spirit ('nul esprit n'existe en ces immensités), and man deprived of his share in that spirit ('je me sens tout seul').

Yet the fact that the tercets offer us questions leaves open the possibility that God still lives. Moreover the proposition that God may have power to conquer death is placed alongside the question 'est-ce toi que je sens en moi-même?', suggesting that if God does still exist, it must be *within* Christ. Christ's belief in God's existence within himself would, it seems, be enough to maintain the existence of God. It is not a matter of fact, but of faith. The words do not assert this, because since the questions remain unanswered and unanswerable, there are no grounds for definite assertion. The statement 'Hélas! et si je meurs, c'est que tout va mourir!' echoes the 'Tout est mort!' of the second sonnet: if Christ dies, it will mean the death of the god within him, and therefore of everything. But there is this difference: '*si* je meurs' offers the possibility that the *haleine immortelle* of the second quatrain may in truth be immortal, that perhaps Christ will not die eternally. The sonnet thus ends with the desperate possibility of the death of all things, beyond which we can, however, detect a desperate hope. It is a hope as apparently irrational as the presence of the rainbow at the end of the second sonnet. There is no more *reason* for Christ to maintain his faith in God than there is for him to believe that God will offer him pardon; but this Christ is still talking to God.

IV. The fourth sonnet (p. 52) picks up the narrative again, and begins with what looks like an answer to the questions of the third: 'Nul n'entendait gémir l'éternelle victime'. At the beginning of the poem, Christ addresses the disciples; when they sleep on and do not hear him (cf. Matthew, xxvi, 40), he continues to speak as if to himself, until in the third sonnet he begins to address first the *puissance originelle*, and then more specifically *mon père*. None of all these, it seems, is listening to him. It should be noted however that while Vigny in 'Le Mont des Oliviers' assumes that God is present but unwilling to answer, maintaining what Vigny calls the 'silence éternel de la Divinité', Nerval's poem suggests rather that God is powerless to act, is no longer really present at all: 'Aurais-tu succombé... Car je me sens tout seul...' (III, ll. 11 and 13). With his last remaining strength, therefore, Christ turns to 'le *seul*—éveillé dans Solyme' (Solyma or Hierosolyma, the Latin name for Jerusalem), to the only power he has not yet called upon: Judas. Christ addresses Judas as a friend (cf. Matthew, xxvi, 50), and asks him to end his suffering quickly (cf. John, xiii, 27) by selling him for what he is worth. The powers of good can no longer help him, but Judas offers an alternative: 'la force du crime'. Judas, with his *noirceurs*, is the representative of the 'ange des nuits', an agent of darkness. If God can do nothing for Christ, perhaps the force that has conquered God can help him?

But the solution is not to be so simply found.

... Judas s'en allait, mécontent et pensif,

Se trouvant mal payé, plein d'un remords si vif

Qu'il lisait ses noirceurs sur tous les murs écrites ...

We are reminded momentarily of 'Vers Dorés': 'Crains, dans le mur aveugle, un regard qui t'épie ...' Judas is not the splendid dark angel that Christ had imagined. He is a man, weak and entirely human, discontented with the price he has been paid for an act that troubles his conscience, and afraid of retribution. He does not possess *la force du crime* at all. The positive force of evil is no more a verifiable reality than is the positive power of good.

It is left for the final tercet to form the only logical conclusion:

Enfin Pilate seul, qui veillait pour César,

Sentant quelque pitié, se tourna par hasard:

«Allez chercher ce fou!» dit-il aux satellites.[67]

We are back in the universe with which the third sonnet began, whose governing principle is mere chance, neither good nor evil. Pilate's action is based on an impulse which seems good, and he, not Judas, proves to be *le seul*, who brings about the good which Christ desired, the end of suffering. But there is no inherent system of cause and effect: good is not the reward for good (Pilate regards Christ as 'ce fou'), but a casual impulse which is good *by chance*. We have thus progressed to the point where the poet, uncertain whether the universe is governed by good or evil, unable to believe in the absolute power of either God or devil, is reduced to seeing the universe as a cosmic accident. The fourth sonnet here ends the narrative proper, leaving the final sonnet to comment on the story.

V. The fifth sonnet (p. 53) reaffirms Pilate's view of Christ as a madman, but it sees his madness as ennobling: 'ce fou, cet insensé sublime ...' Christ is compared to those figures in Greek and Roman mythology who dared, like Christ, to measure themselves against 'la voûte éternelle'. Icarus flew too near the sun and was drowned in the sea when his waxen wings melted in the heat. Phaeton, the son of Apollo, presumed to drive the sun-god's chariot and failed to control it. Atys is a more complex figure, in whom the significance of these images is made clear. The goddess Cybele, his mother, was responsible for his death;[68] full of remorse, she wept for him before Jupiter, and Jupiter granted her a miracle: Atys would never be touched by decay, and every part of his mutilated body would live for ever. Cybele turned him into a pine tree, whose foliage sleeps but does not die in winter; and the earth-goddess wakens him to new life with every spring. Atys, like Horus (for whom Isis puts on *la robe de Cybèle*), is a symbol of the eternal renewal of life, which dies to be reborn.

The three figures, Icarus, Phaeton and Atys, are here made to seem equivalent to each other. There is a hint in the first sonnet of this sequence, as we have seen, that Christ is being punished for his temerity, and like Icarus, through the very knowledge his temerity has gained for him. In this first quatrain, *remontait*, *ranime* suggest resurrection or rebirth, but *perdu sous la foudre des dieux* suggests punishment and annihilation. It is thus probable that a recurring pattern of death followed by rebirth is intended, like that symbolised in the various myths concerning Atys and Cybele. The words 'c'était bien lui' suggest the recognition of a well-known pattern, and the description of Christ in the fourth sonnet as 'l'*éternelle* victime' seems to imply the constant recurrence of that pattern. The original version of this poem has 'la *céleste* victime', a phrase which is echoed in *Isis* (first published 1845; I, 303—the italics are mine):

Pourquoi celui qu'on cherche et qu'on pleure s'appelle-t-il ici Osiris, plus loin Adonis, plus loin Atys? Et pourquoi une autre clameur qui vient du fond de l'Asie cherche-t-elle aussi dans les grottes mystérieuses les restes d'un dieu immolé? Une femme divinisée, mère, épouse ou amante, baigne de ses larmes ce corps saignant et défiguré, victime d'un principe hostile qui triomphe par sa mort, mais qui sera vaincu un jour! La *victime céleste* est représentée par le marbre ou la cire, avec ses chairs ensanglantées, avec ses plaies vives, que les fidèles viennent toucher et baiser pieusement. Mais le troisième jour tout change: le corps a disparu, l'immortel s'est révélé; la joie succède aux pleurs, l'espérance renaît sur la terre; c'est la fête renouvelée de la jeunesse et du printemps.

The linking of Christ with figures from classical and pre-classical mythologies and religions is typical of Nerval's thought. In *Isis* he further explores the likenesses between the mother-and-child images of Isis and Horus, Venus and Eros, Demeter and Bacchus, and the Virgin with the infant Jesus (I, 302–3). Heine, in his poem 'Les Dieux grecs' in *Nordsee* (the translation is Nerval's) regards the dying gods with 'une sainte pitié et une ardente compassion' (it is a feeling we shall find again in 'Horus'); and in the preface to *Les Filles du Feu* Nerval's Brisacier senses the numinous even in the figures of the conventional drama: 'Ne jouons plus avec les choses saintes, même d'un peuple et d'un âge éteints depuis si longtemps, car il y a peut-être quelque flamme encore sous les cendres des dieux de Rome!' (I, 156). There was a great deal of interest in comparative mythology in Nerval's time. Joseph de Maistre in *Les Soirées de Saint-Pétersbourg* (1821) undertook to show that 'les traditions antiques sont toutes vraies', being only 'vérités corrompues et déplacées'; Lammenais in his *Essai sur l'Indifférence en matière de religion* (1817–23) offered a similar argument; Ballanche in his *Orphée* (1827–9) stressed that the ancient myths were symbolic representations of the *vérités primitives*. In Nerval's case such beliefs were founded not merely in theoretical arguments but in an emotional need; he could not accept the triumph of Jehovah over the pagan gods (cf. 'Antéros'), nor that of Christianity over the gods of Greece and Rome (cf. 'Delfica' and 'Myrtho'), and liked to think that salvation would be extended to everything that the human spirit had ever regarded as holy: 'Il serait si beau d'absoudre et d'arracher aux malédictions éternelles les héros et les sages de l'antiquité!' (*Isis*; I, 302).

The figures with whom Christ is linked in this final sonnet are symbolic of the cyclical return of spring, underlining the fact that death is not an end, but the necessary condition for the resurrection of life. It should be noted that even before his crucifixion, Christ undergoes a symbolic death. His punishment begins not with his arrest, but with his presumption:

> J'ai touché de mon front à la voûte éternelle;
> Je suis sanglant, brisé, souffrant pour bien des jours!

Deliverance comes only at the point where he is reduced to helplessness ('sans force penché') and stretched upon the ground ('sur la terre couché'). The poem seems to affirm that some kind of acceptance of weakness and suffering, some kind of abnegation which is in its way a death of the individual, is the necessary prelude to deliverance and rebirth. The figure of Prometheus is not far from the poet's mind in this passage (see Introduction), and there is a curious parallel with the passage in Heine's *De l'Allemagne*[69] in which the philosopher Fichte is compared to the Titan Prometheus: 'Le Titan idéaliste qui, avec l'échelle des pensées, avait escaladé le ciel, et d'une main téméraire avait plongé dans le vide céleste, devient maintenant quelque chose de courbé, d'humblement chrétien, qui soupire beaucoup d'amour'. 'Tu sais ce qu'on m'estime . . .'; there is a genuine humility in Christ's call to Judas. The notion would link this poem with 'Vers Dorés', for humility is what 'libre penseur' conspicuously lacks, and the utter helplessness of Christ is reminiscent of the passive element stressed in the words 'à la nature éclose' in 'Vers Dorés.'

The second quatrain hangs breathlessly over the mystery: the augur tries to read the future in the body of the sacrifice, and the whole universe seems about to fall apart.[70] The old gods appear to have given up their power to this new god. But it is only for 'un instant': are they then not to die for ever? will they be reborn in their turn? As Christ continued to speak to God, so Caesar continues to ask for answers from Jupiter,[71] who is obviously not dead in Caesar's eyes; and Caesar, like Christ, suggests that the victorious power may be not god but devil: 'si ce n'est un dieu, c'est au moins un démon . . .' We are thus offered again all the possibilities which the first four sonnets have considered. And we are left, finally, without an answer. Indeed, there will never be an answer: 'l'oracle invoqué pour jamais dut se taire'. Only one being could have answered: 'Celui qui donna l'âme aux enfants du limon'.[72] It looks at first sight like an answer in itself; but nothing *in the poem* allows us to identify this being: we have been offered, with apparently equal chances, the God of Christ or of Caesar, the devil, and blind 'hasard'.

The poem, then, is finally inconclusive, a characteristic it shares with others of *Les Chimères*. Certain conclusions, however, can clearly be drawn. It is decidedly not the work of a convinced atheist; the possibility that there may be no god, no beneficent spirit informing the universe, is a source of anguish: 'Pleurez! enfants, vous n'avez plus de père!' This view remained unchanged throughout Nerval's life. In 'Quintus Aucler' (II, 1186) [73] he deplores the atheistic tendencies of his times, and perhaps even more, his contemporaries' apparent indifference to religion, which leads them to restore the ruined tombs of Saint-Denis not out of piety but 'par amour de l'art et de la symétrie'. Antagonism is at least meaningfully engaged with its object; it affirms the existence of what it tries to fight. But modern man denies God by his indifference: 'avec le scepticisme de notre époque, on frémit parfois de rencontrer tant de portes sombres ouvertes sur le néant'. That *néant* is what Nerval most fears, and it appears in 'Le Christ aux Oliviers' in the image of the 'puits sombre': 'Seuil de l'ancien chaos dont le néant est l'ombre'. Despite all the difficulties of belief, Nerval could not live without the hope which belief allows; so that like his own image of Christ, he never broke off his dialogue with God.

VERS DORÉS

This sonnet (p. 54) was first published, with minor variants only, in *L'Artiste*, 16 March 1845, under the title 'Pensée antique'. It was reprinted, with the present title and in its present form, in *Petits Châteaux de Bohême* (1853), together with 'Le Christ aux Oliviers' and 'Daphné'. On its first appearance in 1845, 'Daphné' had borne the title 'Vers Dorés'; in 1854, it became 'Delfica'.

This poem seems the least obscure of *Les Chimères*. Addressed directly to man in general, it begins, in a rhetorical style, by expounding a single, clearly stated theme, which is summed up in the epigraph: all things have souls; and to this is added the corollary that all things have power to affect man, who must respect the godhead immanent in everything around him. It is not immediately evident in what way this sonnet is related to the group as a whole, but its appearance in *Petits Châteaux de Bohême* in 1853 shows that Nerval thought of it as related at least to 'Le Christ aux Oliviers' and 'Delfica'. Since he placed it at the end of the sequence in 1854, it would also appear that the reader is intended to see it as the poet's final word on the themes of *Les Chimères*.

The epigraph which Nerval attributes to Pythagoras expresses the 'pensée antique' of the original title. G. Le Breton has shown[74] that Nerval's inspiration for this sonnet was the section of Delisle de Sale's *De la philosophie de la nature* (1777) which is entitled 'Les Douze Surprises de Pythagore'; it is to be found in the chapter headed 'Si l'Homme est dans la nature le seul être sensible'. The 'Surprises' are followed by a short section purporting to be a translation of Pythagoras, which Delisle entitles 'Fragment des vers dorés de Pythagore'. Delisle sums up the Pythagorean doctrine as 'le dogme de l'âme universelle', and his text was one of Hugo's sources for 'Le Satyre' (in *La Légende des Siècles*). As with the *Songe* of Jean-Paul, however, what is most interesting, in my view, is the way in which Nerval makes use of what he borrows.

The first quatrain reminds man that he is free to use his powers as he chooses: 'Des forces que tu tiens ta liberté dispose';[75] but there is life in all things, and man, who does not consult the universe before he acts, may not be the only living thing that is capable of thought. Typically, the quatrain sets these ideas side by side, without comment. Yet the fourth line acquires a curious resonance from this juxtaposition:

Mais de tous tes conseils l'univers est absent.

The 'mais' is a rare example of a significant conjunction in *Les Chimères*. One feels that the poet is criticising man for his disregard of other forms of life, or suggesting that man's actions are of limited consequence when seen in this wider context, or ironically chiding man for his presumption in believing himself unique; any or all of these implications may be intended. There seems to be an echo in this quatrain of Pascal's description of man as a 'roseau pensant', whose capacity to think gives him, despite his fragility, a dignity which the rest of the universe lacks. It is thought which sets man above all other created things, says Pascal: 'je ne puis concevoir l'homme sans pensée: ce serait une pierre ou une brute'.[76] Nerval's sonnet rejects this scale of values, finding the hidden god also 'dans la bête' and 'sous l'écorce des pierres', and denying the uniqueness of man's mind: 'te crois-tu seul pensant?' The basis of these ideas is partly the legacy of Pythagoreanism which Nerval shared with many writers of the early nineteenth century; thus in the year in which 'Vers Dorés' was published, Nerval comments that Goethe did not like dogs, but respected them because 'Il s'était fait dans ses derniers jours un système mélangé des rêveries pythagoriciennes et des idées de Leibnitz sur les monades ou molécules animiques . . .' These ideas happened to blend admirably with the beginnings of comparative biology: in the same article Nerval quotes Cuvier's findings on the intelligence of animals.[77] The quatrain is not attempting to deny the dignity of man, but only to put him in his proper place, as one living being in a whole universe of living beings; and it specifically mocks the pretensions of the 'libre penseur', who believes in the autonomy of man's mind and in the superiority of man to other forms of life. In this respect Nerval's poem differs essentially from Hugo's 'Ce que dit la Bouche d'Ombre', with which it has been compared.[78] Hugo thinks not in terms of a brotherhood, but of a hierarchy, which places man very high in the scale of created things. The same is true of Delisle de Sale's text, which speaks of 'une grande échelle . . . bornée à une de ses extrémités par l'Etre Suprême, et à l'autre par les éléments de la matière; le sentiment s'y affaiblit par une dégradation finement nuancée . . .': despite the insistence on the need for man to respect every being at every point of the scale, there is no doubt that in this scheme of things man is nearer to God than animals, plants and stones, in whom 'le sentiment . . . devient sans cesse plus obtus'. Though the Surrealists in general mistook Nerval's method for one resembling their own (see Introduction), André Breton[79] understood the meaning of 'Vers Dorés'. Surrealism, he says, rejects the view that man is superior to all other created things:

> Bien plutôt à cet égard sa position rejoindrait celle de Gérard de Nerval telle qu'elle s'exprime dans le fameux sonnet 'Vers Dorés' . . . c'est seulement en toute humilité que l'homme peut faire servir le peu qu'il sait de lui-même à la reconnaissance de ce qui l'entoure. Pour cela, le grand moyen dont il dispose est l'intuition poétique.

This poetic intuition seems to be at work in Nerval's description of the universe in which man finds himself; each element of creation is presented as individual, different from other beings, yet working with them to form the harmony of the universe. The second quatrain enjoins man to respect the universe around him, because all things have sentient life, and all have power over his being. Man and the universe in which he lives are on an equal footing: he has 'forces', the universe is 'puissant'. The tercets develop this idea, and insist on man's responsibility for the effects that his freedom to act may have on the living things around him; that is to say, the corollary of 'tout sur ton être est puissant' must be 'ton être est puissant sur tout'. Man and the universe are in reciprocal relation to each other. The poem here introduces, not as an abstraction but by means of concrete imagery, the notion that the universe is watching man. Walls have eyes: 'Crains, dans le mur aveugle, un regard qui t'épie'. One is reminded of Baudelaire's 'Correspondances', in which nature observes man 'avec des regards familiers'. The spirit hidden under the bark of stones is likened to an embryonic eye forming behind closed lids (perhaps the sole indication in Nerval's poetry that he was for a time, at his father's wish, a student of medicine). Nerval has fused the notion of the eye of an unborn child with Delisle's 'enveloppe grossière des fossiles', being concerned to stress not merely man's awareness of other beings, but also their awareness of him; in doing so he has transmuted a rather inert image into one of great poetic intensity, and a theoretical idea into a genuine 'intuition poétique' of the life in natural things.

The terms *penseur, pensant, conseils*, incline one to read the word 'esprit' in the fifth line, as 'mind'; the reasoning seems to follow logically: 'animals also think'. However, the sonnet does not make any clear distinction between thought and feeling, mind and soul; the two are simply placed side by side:

> Respecte dans la bête un *esprit* agissant:
> Chaque fleur est une *âme* à la nature éclose . . .

All things are both 'sensible' and 'puissant'. The 'Dieu caché' is thus quite unlike the 'libre penseur', who is all 'esprit' and 'forces'. True life, embodied in whatever form, is at once active (*agissant*) and passive (*à la nature éclose*), both able to act and willing to be acted upon. This extremely important idea is here stated somewhat obliquely; yet there is certainly implicit in 'Vers Dorés' a recognition that the mind of man is the possible flaw in the system. It is he who is likely, through mistaken pride in his power of thought, to forget or to be unaware of the respect he owes to other forms of life. Such an attitude is a sin against the principle embodied in matter:

> A la matière même un verbe est attaché . . .
> Ne la fais pas servir à quelque usage impie!

The 'verbe' is the Word-made-flesh of the New Testament (though the idea goes back to the Logos of the Greek philosophers). Matter, like man himself, is a manifestation of God's spirit in visible form. It is evidently a blasphemy to attempt to deal with God, or with created things, on the basis of reason alone. Nerval recognised that the legacy of the eighteenth century's belief in the supremacy of reason was the greatest single factor impeding his acceptance of God's power (see Introduction). Intelligence alone is not enough. Worse, salvation demands a perfect faith and a total self-surrender, like that required of Christ in 'Le Christ aux Oliviers'; and intelligence is likely to block even the most genuine urge to submit.

Yet even if man succeeds in resolving this conflict, there may still be something to fear. The implications of the quatrains link this poem at once with 'Le Christ aux Oliviers', and it becomes apparent why Nerval published them together in 1853. If all things have life and exist in reciprocal relation to each other, the whole system can only be tolerable if the principle informing it is a principle of good. In an undirected universe such as Christ sees in his visions, or in one dominated by 'la force du crime', the principle 'tout sur ton être est puissant' would be horrifying. To be acceptable, the interaction of the forms of life must be mutually respectful and mutually beneficial. Hence the injunction to man: 'Respecte . . .'; and hence the assertion, implicit in the parallel construction of the fifth, sixth and seventh lines, that *esprit* and *âme* are equivalent to 'un mystère d'amour'. Love is the force that links lives together, enhances life and creates new life. It allows man an active part in the universe: he can help to create its unity.

It is not difficult to see, however, that since love is a two-way relationship, man cannot fully control its action: the part cannot dominate the whole. Love is literally 'un mystère', a sacrament in which, as in the religious mysteries, a man can participate if he will, but which he can never fully comprehend. Christ too would like to be given the answers to his questions; but it is only when he is 'sans force' that he is granted death and resurrection. Man must be prepared not only to act, but to accept in all simplicity the notion that the life outside him has power in its turn to act on him. If he merely accepts with his intelligence the dignity of beast and stone, he has only won half the battle: he must allow his soul, like that of the flower, to be 'à la nature éclose'. Only thus can he achieve a true participation in the life of the universe.

What this sonnet does not describe is the nature of that participation, or what it might feel like to abandon self in order to be part of something greater than self. Such a state is described in *Aurélia* (I, 403–4):

Du moment que je me fus assuré de ce point que j'étais soumis aux épreuves de l'initiation sacrée, une force invincible entra dans mon esprit. Je me jugeais un héros vivant sous le regard des dieux; tout dans la nature prenait des aspects nouveaux, et des voix secrètes sortaient de la plante, de l'arbre, des animaux, des plus humbles insectes, pour m'avertir et m'encourager . . . les objets sans formes et sans vie se prêtaient eux-mêmes aux calculs de mon esprit;—des combinaisons de cailloux, des figures d'angles, de fentes ou d'ouvertures, des découpures de feuilles, des couleurs, des odeurs et des sons, je voyais ressortir des harmonies jusqu'alors inconnues. 'Comment, me disais-je, ai-je pu exister si longtemps hors de la nature et sans m'identifier à elle? Tout vit, tout agit, tout se correspond; les rayons magnétiques émanés de moi-même ou des autres traversent sans obstacle la chaîne infinie des choses créées . . .'

This passage is so beautiful, and so reminiscent of Baudelaire's 'Correspondances', that the implications of its doctrine are generally missed, although Nerval himself goes on to consider them at once:

Aussitôt je frémis en songeant que ce mystère même pouvait être surpris. 'Si l'électricité, me dis-je, qui est le magnétisme des corps physiques, peut subir une direction qui lui impose des lois, à plus forte raison des esprits hostiles et tyranniques peuvent asservir les intelligences . . . On l'a dit justement: rien n'est indifférent, rien n'est impuissant dans l'univers; un atome peut tout dissoudre, un atome peut tout sauver!

O terreur! voila l'éternelle distinction du bon et du mauvais . . .'
Man has no alternative, if he is truthful, but to recognise that he is a part of a great whole and of no more importance than any other part. Such a recognition can bring him the most profound of joys; but it can also awaken the most helpless terror, 'la crainte d'être à jamais classé parmi les malheureux' (I, 404). The words 'à jamais' are meant to be taken literally, for man's link with the earth does not end with his human life, but persists to all eternity, forever good or forever evil: 'la terre est elle-même un corps matériel dont la somme des esprits est l'âme. La matière ne peut pas plus périr que l'esprit, mais elle peut se modifier selon le bien et selon le mal' (I, 368).

The fear which the poet admits in *Aurélia*, and which is clear in 'Le Christ aux Oliviers', is less obvious in 'Vers Dorés'. It finds expression in words which are in no way emphasised, but whose implications are clear enough: 'crains . . . un regard qui t'épie . . . un Dieu caché . . .' The hidden god may be a principle of life, or a malevolent spirit which watches and waits. Participation in something greater than self can be thought of either as ennoblement or as annihilation. This sonnet makes it plain that Nerval is aware of both possibilities.

DELFICA

This poem (p. 47) has close links with 'Myrtho', although separated from it in the 1854 edition. A manuscript in the collection of M. Dumesnil de Gramont contains a sonnet entitled à 'J-y Colonna', which has the quatrains of 'Delfica' (with minor variants) and the tercets of 'Myrtho'; another manuscript in the same collection contains a sonnet entitled 'Myrtho' which has the quatrains of the present 'Myrtho' and the tercets of 'Delfica'.[80]

This text was first published, substantially in its present form, in *L'Artiste*, 28 December 1845; it bore the title 'Vers Dorés' (later transferred to the sonnet which now bears that name), the date 'Tivoli, 1843', and the epigraph (from Vergil, 'Fourth Eclogue'): *Ultima Cumœi venit jam carminis œtas.* The sonnet was published again, with minor changes which bring it nearer to its final form, in *Petits Châteaux de Bohême* (1853); the title was altered to 'Daphné' and the epigraph (from the same Eclogue) to *Jam redit et virgo* . . .[81] The poem from which the epigraphs were taken predicts the return of a lost Golden Age of peace and prosperity, which is to be heralded by the birth of a child. This Eclogue was obviously much in Nerval's mind early in 1845, for he quotes from it in an article, 'Le Bœuf gras', published in *L'Artiste*, 9 February 1845 (II, 1238), where he speaks of 'le retour de cet âge d'or vanté par les aïeux'. Vergil was doubtless referring to the expected birth of the heir of his patron Pollio; but long tradition regarded this Eclogue as a prediction of the coming of Christ—a fact of which Nerval was surely aware, since school textbooks commonly stress it. Perhaps he realised that he might appear to be attaching a Christian significance to the epigraphs. Such an interpretation is possible for the final lines of 'à Madame Aguado' (see note 80), but it clashes oddly with those of 'Delfica'. At any rate, in 1853 the epigraph is no longer prophetic, and might be taken as a purely personal reference to a particular girl; while in 1854 it is banished entirely. [82]

The first quatrain of this sonnet asks a simple question, in the present tense: 'La connais-tu, DAFNÉ, cette ancienne romance . . .' The word *romance* can be interpreted in two ways. It means 'a song', usually a tender or melancholy song, in regular stanzas, with a simple melody— the 'chanson d'amour' of the fourth line. More specifically, the term is applied, in the Middle Ages, to popular poems in the Romance languages, which dealt, often in dialogue form, with historical or sentimental subjects. In Spain, a number of short romances on heroic or legendary themes would be grouped together and called a Romancero—the *Romancero del mio Cid* is an example. The romance in 'Delfica' is very old: 'cette ancienne romance'; the word *ancienne* implies that the song of which the poet speaks belongs as much to the past as to the present. The fourth line defines it further as 'Cette chanson d'amour *qui toujours recommence*'. The song, then, is eternally renewed, and thus belongs to past, present and future alike.

The second quatrain adds a second, similar question, again in the present tense; but this time the verb is '*Re*connais-tu . . .' The Temple is something which Dafné may recognise because she has seen it before: the imperfect tense of *s'imprimaient* indicates an actual past. The action of memory offers evidence of the continuity of past and present time in the life of one human being: the past is not dead, since it can be re-created in the present; the present is seen to be an extension of the past, not a cancellation of it.

The second part of this quatrain, although linked with the first by the simple conjunction *et*, suddenly alters the perspective. Instead of questioning, the voice seems to be reflecting, and from the personal plane we move abruptly to the world of myth. The present tense *dort* combined with the adjective *antique* produces the same effect as the combination of *ancienne* and the present tense in the first quatrain: these two lines refer to something that was, and still is, though in a dormant state. We will examine presently what that something may be; the reader of this sonnet has barely time to note the legendary quality of the *dragon vaincu* and the suggestion of danger in *fatale* and *imprudents*, as the poem moves forward insistently to the end of the quatrains. It should be noted how this forward movement is accelerated by the simplicity of the syntactical structure, and by the use of two rhymes containing the same sound *an* or *en*, echoed internally by *an*cienne, tr*em*blants, ch*an*son, t*em*ple, *an*tique, so that the musical phrase, as well as the sense, carries one forward to the end of the eighth line.

At this point, it must be mentioned that the two quatrains of this sonnet, as Gilbert Rouger has pointed out,[83] bear a striking resemblance to the 'Chanson de Mignon' from Goethe's *Wilhelm Meister*, or rather to an adaptation of Goethe's poem by Toussenel which was published by Nerval in his *Second Faust* (1840). In one detail at least ('der Drachen alte Brut': 'du dragon . . . l'antique semence') Nerval's sonnet seems to me to be nearer to Goethe's poem than to Toussenel's version:

> Connais-tu la contrée où dans le noir feuillage
> Brille comme un fruit d'or le fruit du citronnier
> Où le vent d'un ciel bleu rafraîchit sans orage
> Les bocages de myrte et les bois de laurier? . . .
> Connais-tu la maison, le vaste péristyle
> Et la sombre caverne où dort le vieux serpent? . . .

This similarity raises in acute form the problem of literary sources discussed in the Introduction. The reference to Goethe's lyric, *if the reader recognises it*, adds to 'Delfica' that nostalgia for a place of warmth and love which is the theme of Mignon's song. But 'Delfica' contains both these and other elements, which the reader can perceive even if he does not know Mignon's song; and it is precisely what Nerval has added to his model that must concern us.

The forward movement of the poem culminates, at the point where reference to Goethe's poem ends, in the confident assertion of the first tercet: 'Ils reviendront ces dieux que tu pleures toujours!' The future tense appears as the logical completion of the sequence of time already established in the quatrains: what was, and is now dormant, will be again; the link between future and past is made clearer by 'le temps *va ramener* l'ordre des *anciens* jours'. No doubt whatever is expressed of the certainty of this renewal; moreover the poet has received a physical sign to confirm it: 'La terre a tressailli d'un souffle prophétique . . .'[84]

At this triumphant climax there is a pause. When the voice begins again, it is with the word *Cependant*, and a return to the present: 'Cependant la sibylle . . . est endormie encor . . .' The verb recalls the *dort* of the second quatrain. The future triumph, we are reminded, will be, but is not yet. The final line opposes an apparently immovable obstacle to the forward sweep of the poem; *le sévère portique* stands in stern contrast to the brilliant landscape surrounding *le TEMPLE, au péristyle immense*.

Only the one word *encor* reminds us that time is not static: what is, must in time give way to what will be.

In *Petits Châteaux de Bohême* (1853), 'Delfica' appears to represent the culmination of the ideas discussed in 'Le Christ aux Oliviers' and 'Vers Dorés', and to offer, as they do, an affirmation of the reality of rebirth, and of the continuance of life through patterns of death and renewal: by linking these three poems under the title *Mysticisme*, Nerval draws attention to their likeness. Only by seeing 'Delfica' in the context of *Les Chimères* as a group can we observe the underlying complexity of this sonnet, especially in its relation to 'Myrtho', 'Horus' and 'Antéros'. It is not as simple a poem as it at first appears, and its richness of meaning is reflected in its verbal structure, which is very much more dense and elaborate than that of 'Le Christ aux Oliviers' or 'Vers Dorés'. Both musically, in its use of patterns of sound, and visually, in its use of concrete imagery, 'Delfica' seems far more consciously worked than any of Nerval's previous poems, with a new tightness of construction in which the patterns become part of the meaning. We have already noted how the movement of the quatrains is speeded by the repeated use of *an* and *en* sounds. The unity of the sonnet is reinforced by the presence of these same sounds in the tercets, but the effect is subtly changed. In the first tercet the parallel structure of the three lines produces a mounting excitement, in which the echoes of *temps* and *anciens* serve to smooth the way to the acuteness of the climax in the eleventh line, with its sharp internal assonance: tressaill*i*, prophét*i*que. In the second tercet the same vowel sound appears to dominate: s*i*bylle, v*i*sage, endorm*i*e, r*i*en, port*i*que; but there is an undercurrent of echoes from the earlier pattern, which has a curiously lulling effect, suggesting the rhythms of sleep: Cepend*an*t, *en*dormie, *en*cor, Const*an*tin, dér*an*gé. Many other internal rhymes help to create a very close-knit pattern: péristyle, sibylle; antique, prophétique, portique; anciens, rien, latin, Constantin; chanson, citrons, dragon, reviendront (these last at the beginnings of lines, so that there is a rhyme at both ends of the line, as it were). The total effect of this richness of musically orchestrated sound is to dull the reader's perception of the sense and to produce only a vague apprehension of a landscape and a mood. This may be why 'Delfica' was published in 1845 while 'Myrtho' and 'Horus', which are much more explicit, were not. Its complexities of meaning are hidden beneath a surface which appears to present no asperities of any kind. Perhaps no further development along these lines seemed possible or desirable. Certainly 'Delfica' is the only poem in *Les Chimères* to exploit the effects of formal pattern to this extent.

The complexity of 'Delfica' is revealed only when one looks closely at its images, prising them out, for this purpose, from their protective setting. They then appear in no way simple or unequivocal. Character-istic of the imaginative syntheses of this poem are the linked images of the cave, the dragon and the Sibyl. The Latin Sibyls were priestesses of Apollo, like the Delphic Pythia. The most famous of them was the Cumaean Sibyl, whose home was in a cave at Cumae, near Naples; it was she who guided Aeneas on his journey to the Underworld. (The *prêtresse au visage vermeil* of 'à Madame Aguado' and 'Erythréa' is the more ancient Erythrean Sibyl of Asia Minor, with whom the Cumaean Sibyl was later often identified: her name is derived from the Greek word meaning 'red': hence 'vermeil'.) The dragon, however, belongs to the traditions of Delphi in Greece. The Python, a serpent or dragon, guarded the ancient sanctuary of Themis, and was slain by Apollo, who took the sanctuary for his own, and gave his priestess the name of Pythia. Another link with Apollo is the name Daphne, which was at one point the title of this sonnet. Daphne was the nymph who fled from Apollo's love; to save her, her father the river-god turned her into a laurel-tree. The laurel was Apollo's emblem; and in the last of the oracles pronounced at Delphi for the Emperor Julian, the death of the cult was symbolised in the phrase: 'the laurel of his divination is withered'. Daphne is also the name of a place connected with the Emperor Julian and his attempt to renew the cult of Apollo.

However, the words 'du dragon vaincu . . . l'antique semence' raise a problem. The 'dragon's seed' suggests the race of Thebans sprung from the teeth of the dragon slain by Cadmus—this is presumably the legend referred to in a verse of 'Antéros':

Je ressème à ses pieds les dents du vieux dragon.

The connection of the dragon's seed with the Sibyl or with Apollo is tenuous, unless Nerval is thinking of the Pythia as being in some way the child of the Python. It seems likely that this is an example of imaginative synthesis: the prediction of the rebirth of the cult of Apollo, who is already connected with a dragon, suggests to the poet the theme of rebirth symbolised by the legend of the dragon's teeth. In his play *Léo Burckart* (1839), Nerval likens the revolutionary spirit in Europe to 'ce héros antique qui semait les dents du dragon'.[85] In 'Quintus Aucler', a phrase recalling the images of 'Delfica' links the notion of rebirth (renaissance) with the beginnings of a return to the old gods in the fifteenth century: 'Le *palladium mystique*, qui avait jusque-là protégé la ville de Constantin, allait se rompre, et déjà la semence nouvelle faisait sortir de terre les génies emprisonnés du vieux monde' (II, 1209).

This last image links the classical gods with the race of Cain, who are also 'génies emprisonnés'. The early version of this poem ('à J-y Colonna'; I, 13) has 'serpent' instead of 'dragon'. In the *Carnet de Notes du Voyage en Orient* (II, 713–14), Nerval refers to the ancient belief that Cain was the son of Eve and the Serpent, and links the 'vieille race du serpent' with a mountain cave: 'Elie Grotte' (Elie is the ancient Mount Taygetus in the Peloponnese; Nerval mentions it in the *Voyage en Orient*: 'la vue du Taygète lointain comme l'apparition d'un dieu'; II, 67). The race of Cain, defeated by Jehovah, are the 'Fils du Feu', descended from Tubal-Kain, the god of fire who appears in Nerval's *Voyage en Orient*. We shall meet the god of fire again in 'Horus'; and in 'Antéros', Jehovah is defied by one who likens himself to Cain. His description of himself as having 'sur un col flexible une tête indomptée' may not immediately suggest a serpent, but the words are echoed in Nerval's description of a dance that he saw performed in Constantinople, in which the leader of a chain of linked dancers 'semblait la tête au col flexible d'un serpent' (*Voyage en Orient*; II, 458—this chapter was first published in 1850). The seed of the 'serpent vaincu', the sons of Cain, are a superior race of artists and poets. In their cave-like home in the heart of the mountain of Kaf they await the defeat of Jehovah and the return of a golden age.

The journey to the golden age will not be achieved without courage, for there are dangers to be faced, as the word *fatale* implies.[86] We are not clearly told what these dangers might be, but the fact that both Cadmus and Apollo were obliged to do battle with a monster before the new order which they represented could be established, links the theme of the dragon with the initiation rites of the ancient mysteries. The mysteries are discussed by Nerval in *Isis*, one of the pieces in *Les Filles du Feu* (and the goddess Isis appears in 'Horus'); and in another of these stories, *Octavie*, he tells of a visit to a temple of Isis at Pompeii, near Naples, where he and Octavie re-enacted the ceremonies of the cult. Initiates were obliged to undergo a series of trials, some of which involved physical danger; in *Voyage en Orient* (II, 225*ff.*) Nerval discusses the theory that the subterranean chambers of the Pyramids were used for this purpose. A Pyramid in the plain of Gizeh is also named as the refuge of the last of the race of Cain during the Flood (II, 564–5), and Tubal-Kain stresses the courage and perseverance they required to reach the haven underground, and the equal dangers they faced when they made the journey back to the surface of the earth: only Tubal-Kain and his son survived. The myth of Orpheus is also related to the rites of the Pyramids (II, 230–1); and Aeneas's journey to the Underworld, following the instructions of the Sibyl of Cumae, belongs to the same tradition.

In *Voyage en Orient* (II, 569) Nerval compares the descent of the artist Adoniram, a son of the race of Cain, into the heart of the mountain of Kaf, to 'la descente d'Enée aux enfers'. Moreover, in *Aurélia* (I, 414) he uses this term of his own spiritual crises: 'je compare cette série d'épreuves que j'ai traversées à ce qui, pour les anciens, représentait l'idée d'une descente aux enfers'; and in 'El Desdichado' the poet likens himself to

Orpheus, who also made a journey to the Underworld. Legend and myth, it is clear, are not being used as sources of decorative images, but because they express an aspect of the poet's own experience.

In 'Delfica', Nerval refers to ideas which he discusses in detail in 'Quintus Aucler' (first published *Revue de Paris*, November 1851), one of the studies grouped together in *Les Illuminés* (1852).[87] Nerval describes the renewal of neo-Platonic ideals at the time of the French Revolution, and sees in this renewal a justification of the beliefs of the Emperor Julian (A.D. 331–363). Julian, known as 'the Apostate', abjured his Christian faith, and tried to reverse the policy of his uncle Constantine and to restore the cult of the ancient gods in the Roman Empire. In the following passage Nerval proclaims 'le retour cyclique des destinées qui rendaient la victoire au divin empereur' (II, 1208; the Latin quotation is again from Vergil's Fourth Eclogue:

—Les vers sibyllins avaient prédit mille fois ces évolutions rénovatrices, depuis le *Redeunt Saturnia regna* jusqu'au dernier oracle de Delphes, qui, constatant le règne millénaire de Iacchus-Iésus, annonçait aux siècles postérieurs le retour vainqueur d'Apollon.

In the original publication of 'Quintus Aucler' a variant of two lines of 'Delfica' follows:

Ils reviendront, ces dieux que tu pleures toujours,

Le temps ramènera l'ordre des anciens jours.

If we now go back to examine the images used in this sonnet, we should be able to define more clearly what it is whose eternity is being celebrated here. The most obvious group of images links the romance of which the poet speaks with the world of antiquity. The word *ancienne* suggests that the 'romance' is not only a song of love, but one which has a legendary background: and the adjective is given a specific content by means of the imagery of the quatrains, so that when it recurs in 'l'ordre des *anciens* jours', we know what kind of world the poet has in mind. That world is not clearly identified with classical Greece, despite the title 'Delfica' and the name Dafné; the sibyl's *visage latin* suggests that Rome is as much in the poet's mind as Greece. A vaguely legendary rather than a classical quality is felt in the image of the *dragon vaincu*, as well as in the word *romance*. Though we may know that a dragon once occupied the site of the Delphic oracle, *in its place in the poem* the image seems mysterious, and carries with it a host of references to familiar myths and stories: Jason and the Golden Fleece, Hercules and the Hydra, and perhaps also the whole company of mediaeval dragons; chiefly we are aware at this point of a hint of dangers to be overcome in the search for a great prize. A further suggestion of the marvellous appears in the prophetic trembling of the earth. The ancient world, in fact, is an atmosphere, and evoked chiefly through its landscape.

The scene is set for us first with the five kinds of trees named in the first quatrain, with the Temple, and the lemons. All of these still exist in the present time, and all of them are generally Mediterranean in feeling, rather than specifically classical. We might even be in Provence. The landscape is evoked with a remarkable economy of means. The Mediterranean atmosphere suggests warmth and light, though these are not mentioned at all: olive and myrtle carry with them the colours of the south. The laurel trees may be white-flowered, but *blancs* suggests also the reflected brilliance of the Mediterranean sun. The trembling of the willow trees adds movement and life to the image, and perhaps suggests again the shimmering light; it echoes also the trembling of the earth: 'La terre a tressailli . . .' The classical Temple stands, not solidly on the ground, but soaring upwards in the expansion of two nasal vowels: 'le Temple au péristyle immense'.

Against all this brilliance, the human figures might easily be lost. But the poet gives the girl a sharp reality in one detail, at the same time adding the physical sensation of taste to the illusion of sight: 'Et les citrons amers où s'imprimaient tes dents'—the consonants seem to bite into the fruit. The girl who ate lemons appears in *Octavie*.[88] The scene of the poet's encounter with Octavie is set largely in and near Naples, where the legendary tomb of Vergil stands under a laurel tree on Posilipo; she is the girl with whom the poet visited the temple of Isis. This incident is also commemorated in 'Myrtho', where the laurel tree is called 'le laurier de Virgile'. If we look for a model for Octavie in real life, we may find her in a letter (I, 791–2) which Nerval wrote in 1834 from Marseille (where we are, in fact, in Provence); but the vivid detail in the sonnet has a significance which does not depend on its reality. Reality, in the sense of accuracy in the recording of facts, is of no consequence. Though the original version of this sonnet is dated 'Tivoli, 1843', Nerval, as far as we know, visited Rome in 1834, but not on his return to Italy in 1843. The poet is concerned to record an experience, and in his mind the experience may well be composed of elements from different times and places, some lived and some imagined. Indeed, the multiple nature of the images in this sonnet derives from just such a fusion: the grotto of the Sirens at Tivoli, seen in 1834, is assimilated to the caves at Naples, and then to the Oriental legends connected with the Pyramids, which the poet saw in 1843. The varied aspects of the *grotte*: dangerous home of the Sirens, place of trial and initiation, and haven of the élite, become one in imagination; so that when Nerval describes the imaginary cave in the mountain of Kaf, in the *Voyage en Orient*, it sounds much like the 'Grotte du chien' at Solfatara near Naples, with its intense heat and sulphurous fumes,[89] and when he describes 'Tivoli' in 'Delfica', it has absorbed the qualities of the legendary 'grotte'. What matters is not the actual place, or the actual event, but its echoes in the poet's mind. Moreover, the power of memory to re-create a lost world, in the same way as legends do, gives the remembered detail symbolic value: the personal human experience acquires the prestige of a myth, and the people involved seem to live on the same plane as legendary heroes and gods, so that it seems perfectly natural that the gods should give them a sign. The song which the girl is asked to recognise is a song of love, but the love belongs not only to one girl and one landscape; it goes beyond them to include the world of antiquity and the gods for whom the girl weeps.

In contrast to the warmth and life of the ancient world, the arch of Constantine, defender of the Christians (Nerval had no doubt seen this monument in Rome), is heavy and unmoving, 'le sévère portique'; its very sound is constricted, reminding one of the 'porte étroite' of the Christian heaven. For the poet it is not a triumphal arch, but the door that bars the way into Alice's garden. Yet despite its nostalgia for 'les dieux' this poem is in no way an absolute rejection of Christianity; both in 'Horus' and in 'Le Christ aux Oliviers' (see commentary on this poem) Nerval shows that he was aware of the many links between the different religions and mythologies he encountered, and that he accepted them all as equally valid. Clearly, however, this poem associates the *chanson d'amour* not with the present era, but with a lost world that exists in the dimension of past time.

When he was in Greece, Nerval saw it at first as unreal: 'Il me semble que je marche au milieu d'une comédie.' Later he realised that he was walking in the childhood of the world, in a place where 'le passé renaît sous l'enveloppe du présent' (*Voyage en Orient*; II, 84). He was enchanted to hear men speak a language which had so long a history, a language moreover which reminded him of the Greek lessons of his schooldays. He was travelling, that is, not in space but in time. Of the various elements of the landscape of 'Delfica', lemons, olives and myrtle are specifically associated with the south, but sycamores, willows and laurels are not. Moreover, the various versions of this sonnet offer alternative trees: 'à J-y Colonna' has mulberries instead of laurels, and the myrtle does not appear; the 1845 version has 'les myrtes en fleur', but no olives.[90] It seems that the landscape is not so much an object in space recalled to memory, as a composite creation; it takes shape slowly, over a period of time; it is formed from the features of landscapes seen or imagined at different times, and the poet gradually becomes aware that some elements are essential to it, others not. The laurel trees are especially interesting. They appear in 1845, are replaced by mulberries in *Petits Châteaux de Bohême*, but are restored at the final revision for publication in *Les Filles du Feu*. In this volume, in the story *Sylvie*, which is full of memories of his childhood in the Valois, Nerval tells how he picked two branches of laurel and fashioned them into a crown for Adrienne (I, 246): 'Je posai sur la tête d'Adrienne cet ornement, dont les feuilles lustrées éclataient sur ses cheveux blonds aux rayons pâles de la lune'. These laurel leaves are white with moonlight; but they are not so far distant from those of the Mediterranean. Nerval describes in *Sylvie* the park at Ermenonville, where he found a little unfinished temple, remembered from his childhood and now almost in ruins, which had 'la forme du temple de la sibylle Tiburtine'. Tibur is the modern Tivoli, whose name accompanies the 1845 version of 'Delfica'. The temple at Ermenonville bore an inscription from Vergil, and was once surrounded by laurel bushes: 'Quant aux lauriers, les a-t-on coupés, comme le dit la chanson des jeunes filles qui ne veulent plus aller au bois? Non, ces arbustes de la douce Italie ont péri sous notre ciel brumeux' (I, 261–2). Like the laurel, and the cult, of Delphi, they could not survive in a hostile climate. Describing his first view of Greece from the ship, Nerval refers (*Voyage en Orient*; II, 67) to the brilliant sunrise, and comments that Homer's Aurora 'aux doigts de rose' never reaches the North: 'Ce que nous autres barbares appelons l'aube ou le point du jour, n'est qu'un pâle reflet, terni par l'atmosphère impure de nos climats déshérités'. The word is the same as that which he uses to describe his times (II, 71): 'ne suis-je pas toujours, hélas! le fils d'un siècle déshérité d'illusions, qui a besoin de toucher pour croire, et de rêver le passé . . . sur ses débris?'; and Nerval's Brisacier, in the preface to *Les Filles du Feu*, describes himself in terms which recall 'El Desdichado': 'le déshérité, le banni de liesse, le beau ténébreux' (I, 152). Both poet and girl in 'Delfica' are *déshérités*; exiles like the laurel trees of Ermenonville, but exiles in time, not in space. The lost golden age is that of Nerval's own childhood, as well as that of legend. 'Nous pensions être en paradis', says Nerval of the children in *Sylvie* (I, 245). The lovers in 'Delfica' are given symbolic value through their links with the world of legend, and they become representative of the human condition. They are Adam and Eve shut out of Paradise, adults cut off from what Baudelaire called 'le vert paradis des amours enfantines', and children of an age deprived of God.

We have seen that the poem ends cautiously. There are in fact no absolute certainties in this poem. To begin with, the quatrains are expressed as questions, not as statements. The poet is asking the girl if she remembers the lost world. The urgency of the movement insists that the answer must surely be yes; but we cannot be certain that it is: perhaps the song means nothing to anyone other than the poet. There is some undefined danger, and the reward is not assured: while the first tercet insists that the golden age will return, the second reminds us that it is only a promise. Moreover, the words *dort* and *endormie* are dangerously equivocal: are these things asleep, or dead?[91] 'Delfica' leaves open the possibility that the weight of Constantine's arch has crushed the sleeping Sibyl. The sonnet, in fact, closes as well as opens with a question, giving one a sense of having returned to the beginning. Further questions suggest themselves. If time is inconstant, how durable will the golden age be, when it does return? And can the individual really return to the age of childhood? It is probable that faith was one of the elements of the childhood paradise; and as Nerval remarked of his nostalgia for the safety and comfort of religious belief: 'L'ignorance ne s'apprend pas' (*Aurélia*; I, 386).[92]

One absolute remains, though it is one we might easily miss in this particular poem—indeed, perhaps the poet is not yet fully aware of it. The love which is the essence of the lost world is perpetuated in the song, 'Cette chanson d'amour qui toujours recommence'. It is the song which gives that world existence in the present, allowing the human mind to make contact with its own previous experience, with the symbolic world of myth and legend, and with the prophetic insights of the poet. Whatever else may be possible or real, the song exists; and being co-extensive with time, it is the only thing which has reality in past, present and future.

MYRTHO

Like 'Delfica', with which it has close links (see commentary on 'Delfica'), 'Myrtho' (p. 44) is related to *Octavie*, one of the stories in *Les Filles du Feu*. The landscape is once again that of the Mediterranean, and again the poet recalls a past experience which links the landscape with a girl. However, the landscape in this poem is less clearly particularised. Still bathed in the dazzling light of 'Delfica', it has here been reduced to the single word *Pausilippe*. We are in the Bay of Naples, whose islands Nerval describes in *Octavie* as 'inondées des feux de l'Orient' (I, 286). The only physical details which add to the picture are the black grapes, and not far away, the volcano. The girl herself has become transfigured; she has a less human, a more mythical quality than the girl in 'Delfica'. Her image is made more distant by the fact that the poem is not addressed directly to her, as 'Delfica' is addressed to Dafné. The poet is remembering and defining her image in his mind: 'Je *pense* à toi, Myrtho . . .' He calls her 'divine enchanteresse', and the adjective is not mere hyperbole, for the description of her makes us think of a pagan deity, or a Bacchante, with clusters of black grapes entwined in her golden hair.[93] Her brow is 'inondé des clartés d'Orient', and while the word *clartés* seems to reflect the dazzling sunlight which plays on the face of Posilipo 'de mille feux brillant', it may mean at the same time the 'wisdom' of the

East. But goddess or no, she has given the poet a supreme contact with a world of enchantment and beauty. The *rimes riches* underline the elements of that world: *enchanteresse, tresse, ivresse, Grèce*.

Although she is more distant than Dafné, Myrtho is not merely the symbol of an abstraction. Other writers in Nerval's time made the pilgrimage to Posilipo to visit Vergil's tomb; Sainte-Beuve mocks the current fashion in his poem 'Italie' (1829)—which uses, incidentally, the rhymes of 'Myrtho':

> Que m'importent à moi les souvenirs antiques . . .
> Et les noms qu'on veut lire au fronton des portiques . . .
>
> Et les temples sous terre, et les urnes d'argile,
> Tous ces objets si vains de si doctes débats?
> Et que m'importe encor le tombeau de Virgile,
> Et l'éternel laurier auquel je ne ne crois pas?

Nerval transforms what was evidently a conventional landscape into one peculiarly his own, by linking it with a personal experience, as he does with all his landscapes. Exactly as in 'Delfica', he brings the girl to life in a single line: 'dans l'éclair furtif de ton œil souriant', where the word *furtif* gives the image a sudden humanity and nearness. The smiling goddess-like figure of Myrtho was present, it seems, when the poet addressed a prayer to Iacchus—and not merely present, but the source of his fervour: 'C'est dans ta coupe aussi que j'avais bu l'ivresse . . .' This is the incident described in *Octavie* (see commentary on 'Delfica', p. 80), for Iacchus (Bacchus) is linked with the cult of Isis; he was one of the gods venerated at Eleusis, where the mysteries of Isis were celebrated, and in *Isis* (I, 299) Nerval describes the statue of Bacchus which he saw among the treasures of the temple, in the museum at Naples. The poet's *ivresse* is thus compounded of mystical inspiration and an impulse of human love, both in some way dependent on his feeling that in this landscape he is in touch with that lost world which he describes in 'Delfica'.

The linking of past and present takes place under the auspices of the poet Vergil, whose laurel tree appears also in 'Delfica', and whose description of the Underworld in the *Æneid* is modelled on the volcanic region around Naples. But in 'Myrtho' Vergil does not appear only as a prophet, as the writer of the Fourth Eclogue announcing the return of the ancient gods. He is a figure representing both antiquity and the art of poetry; and as in 'Delfica', it is poetry, as well as love, that links the writer of this sonnet with the lost world of the Golden Age: 'Car *la Muse* m'a fait l'un des fils de la Grèce'.

In 'Myrtho', however, the Golden Age is no longer located only in the past: it is suggested that it can be made to exist here and now. Time in this sonnet is complex and indivisible. The first quatrain has only one finite verb, which places the action and the image of Myrtho firmly in the present: 'Je *pense* à toi, Myrtho . . .'. Yet since the image is in the poet's mind it has a timeless quality: even if the poem describes Myrtho as the poet has actually seen her, we cannot tell when that might have been, and the first quatrain gives us a sense that this dazzling creature has existed since the birth of time, and will continue to exist to all eternity: the word *divine* removes her from the limitations of human days and years.

The second quatrain refers to a specific incident in the past ('l'on me voyait priant') which seems to have been precipitated by the fervour instilled in the poet by Myrtho's smiling eye: 'C'est dans ta coupe aussi que j'avais bu l'ivresse . . .'; the tense of the verb makes clear the order of events. Yet the pluperfect does not finally give us a sense of being in the past at all, and indeed the tense is the same as in the tenth line, which refers to the events of yesterday. The image of 'ton œil souriant' makes Myrtho seem very near; and the final line of this quatrain brings us back to the present: 'Car la Muse m'a fait l'un des fils de la Grèce'; the perfect tense implies 'I am still (perhaps always) a son of Greece'.

The first tercet again begins in the present tense, and the action, though past, is no further away than yesterday and today: 'C'est qu'hier tu l'avais touché d'un pied agile': yesterday's actions have restored to the volcano the effective life it had in the past, and which it still has, we feel, at the very moment the poet is writing his sonnet.

The second tercet covers a range of time in the same way as the first quatrain. The verb *brisa* pinpoints a violent action in the past; but the ultimate effect of that action has been to produce, from that moment ('*Depuis* qu'un duc normand brisa . . .'), a unity of differing elements. The verb which expresses that unity is placed centrally in the final line of the sonnet, in the timeless present tense: '*Toujours* . . . Le pâle Hortensia *s'unit* au Myrthe vert'.

Where 'Delfica' appears to envisage an eternal cycle of death and renewal, allowing one to hope for the return of a lost paradise, 'Myrtho' seems to be less emotionally involved in any one stage of the cycle; it considers the events of time from a distance great enough to allow the poet to see them as co-existent and equal. The tone of 'Myrtho' is more reflective ('Je *pense* à toi . . .') and more assured ('Je *sais* pourquoi . . .') than that of 'Delfica'. The implications of the notion of time as eternal recurrence have been avoided in this poem: alternation means impermanence, but co-existence guarantees the durability of the dream.

The essence of the dream appears to be the reconciliation embodied in the second tercet, which provides the logical end to the movement of the whole poem. In *Isis* (I, 302–3), Nerval underlines the similarities between the beliefs and customs of the devotees of Isis and those of Christianity; he hastens to add that in doing so he is not concerned to deny the value of any religion:

> Au contraire, aux yeux du philosophe, sinon du théologien, ne peut-il pas sembler qu'il y ait eu, dans tous les cultes intelligents, une certaine part de révélation divine? ... Une évolution nouvelle des dogmes pourrait faire concorder sur certain points les témoignages religieux des divers temps. Il serait si beau d'absoudre et d'arracher aux malédictions éternelles les héros et les sages de l'antiquité!

This passage makes it clear that Nerval is concerned to effect a genuine reconciliation which will ensure the eternal salvation of both the old gods and the new. In 'Myrtho' they are not at war, as 'Delfica' might lead one to suppose; they co-exist ideally in a dimension of time in which past, present and future are one. The cryptic second tercet seems to affirm a synthesis of apparently opposed forces. The 'duc normand' may be Robert Guiscard, conqueror of Southern Italy, who destroyed the Capitol at Rome in 1084, or his brother, Roger II of Normandy, who conquered Naples in 1130. The clay gods which were shattered then (they are Myrtho's gods: '*tes* dieux d'argile') survive in the myrtle which was used, as Nerval tells us in *Voyage en Orient* (II, 70), in the rites of the goddess Venus. The myrtle is now eternally united with the 'pâle Hortensia'. This flower is generally thought to symbolise the modern era, since it is a plant first cultivated in the eighteenth century. In this context, it seems to symbolise particularly the 'new' religion of Christianity, contrasted with pagan religions.[94] This contrast is frequently made by nineteenth-century poets, and it is generally to the disadvantage of Christianity, which is seen as a religion obsessed with death and the after-life, austere and forbidding in its observances as in its ethics. Vigny, like Nerval, was interested in the Emperor Julian's stand as last defender of a more human faith. He proposed to write a work entitled *Daphné*, which survives only as fragments; in one of these, Vigny compares Julian to Lammenais, whose *Essai sur l'Indifférence en matière de religion* (1817–23) calls for a return to active Christianity. Vigny comments: 'Le Christianisme en est donc au point où en était le Polythéisme en 300'; he considers Lammenais to be as doomed to failure as was Julian in his time.[95] In England, Swinburne too was fascinated by the figure of Julian, and uses the word 'pale' which in 'Myrtho' describes the hydrangea, in his paraphrase of the Emperor's dying call to Christ: 'Thou hast conquered, O pale Galilean'.[96] Swinburne compares the pallor of Christ, and the deathly greyness of the Christian world, with the green laurel of Apollo ('Hymn to Proserpine', *Poems and Ballads, First series*, 1866). In 'Myrtho', the pallor of the new growth contrasts sharply with the vigorous green of the myrtle of Venus, goddess of love. As in 'Delfica', the notion of a strong, surviving love is linked with the classical land-scape and the ancient gods. Yet the hydrangea is not rejected; even if we cannot be sure why Nerval chose this particular flower, the verb *s'unit* makes it clear that what matters is the process by which disparate things are brought together and reconciled.

Unfortunately, Nerval found it difficult to accept emotionally the ideal equality of faiths which his reason postulated and his heart desired, and he shows a clear preference, in both 'Delfica' and 'Myrtho', for the ancient gods. It is significant that in *Isis* his comparison of religions is based on the likenesses between Bacchus, child of Demeter, and those other divine children of divine mothers, Horus the son of Isis, and Atys the son of Cybele; and by stressing the fact that Bacchus was called Iacchus-Iesus, he links him to Jesus the son of Mary.[97] His preference for these figures of the mother-goddess is due to his inability, for reasons which he analyses with lucid intelligence in *Aurélia* (see Introduction), to accept the all-powerful Father-God, the Kneph who is mocked in 'Horus', the Jehovah who is defied in 'Antéros', the authoritarian god of Christianity. This problem is of the greatest importance to Nerval, for it complicated not only his religious thinking, but also his human relation-ships. In the incident in *Octavie* which is recalled in 'Myrtho', the narrator finds that the girl has acquired for him the divinity of the goddess, and that she is now beyond his human reach: 'je n'osai lui parler d'amour ... je lui avouai que je ne me sentais plus digne d'elle' (I, 291). In 'Myrtho' the difficulty of loving is explored again through the related problem of the reconciliation of the old gods and the new.

The movement towards the reconciliation effected in the final tercet of the sonnet is implicit in the relations between the various images evoked. The quatrains create a world of beauty, light, warmth, faith, poetry and love, not in these abstract terms but through their descrip-tion of a sunlit landscape in which an ancient god and a muse are the poet's divinities, and a woman smiles at him. Through the fusion of all these things a miraculous portent is granted to the poet: 'Je sais pourquoi là-bas le volcan s'est rouvert ...' The word *rouvert* underlines the fact that the volcano has come *back* to life, has regained its former fire. And it has done so because 'hier tu l'avais touché d'un pied agile': as in 'Delfica', the precise, physical detail makes the abstract notion seem real in human terms. It is the woman who has brought the seemingly dead to life again; and the awakening of the fires of inner earth recalls the sign in 'Delfica': 'La terre a tressailli d'un souffle prophétique', which foretold the return of the Golden Age. The volcano contains the central fire that can be made to flow freely through the power of love and faith.

As such it resembles the mountain of Kaf, in whose depths the race of Cain, the serpent's son, guard the fires whose heat alone can keep the earth alive: 'la grotte . . . Où du dragon vaincu dort l'antique semence'. When Adoniram is guided to this underworld by Tubal-Kaïn (as Aeneas by the Sibyl, and Dante by Vergil), he learns that the jealousy of Adonaï, the god who rejected Cain's offering of love, has prevented the flow of the vital heat towards the surface of the earth, where it ought to be exchanged with that spark of the central fire which Adonaï placed in every man of clay: 'cet échange de principes était la vie sans fin'. But the earth is growing cold because of the failure of love and trust that has made enemies of Adonaï and the race of Cain (*Voyage en Orient*; II, 558–9). Only through the free interchange of warmth can life be restored; fire, that is, is the symbol of love, the element in which opposites are reconciled and the separate united: 'Le pâle Hortensia s'unit au Myrthe vert'.

However, as in 'Delfica', there is in this sonnet a hint of something sinister underlying the light and warmth of the landscape. The miracle of awakening, symbolised by the fires of the volcano, may be the necessary prelude to the free flow of faith and poetry, and the return of the Golden Age, but it also results in a darkening of the sky: 'Et de cendres soudain l'horizon s'est couvert . . .' The image is not further explored, but it can be no coincidence that in the poet's mind it is abruptly connected with an act of physical violence: 'Depuis qu'un duc normand *brisa* tes dieux d'argile . . .'; and though this discordant note is resolved in the final harmony, its presence cannot be ignored. Indeed, harmony may depend in some way on violent action: the syntax allows one to see the final union as a consequence of the Norman soldier's violence: 'Le pâle Hortensia s'unit au Myrthe vert Depuis qu'un duc normand brisa . . .'

There is undoubtedly a danger in the volcano. In *Octavie* the act of love is followed by the eruption of the volcano, and the sulphurous ash of Vesuvius floating over the town makes the poet feel that he is suffocating: 'Une poussière chaude et soufrée m'empêchait de respirer' (I, 290). He leaves the girl sleeping and goes up to Posilipo, his mind full of thoughts of death. In *Les Nuits d'Octobre* and in *La Pandora* there are echoes of this incident, in guilt-ridden nightmares which obviously distressed Nerval profoundly. In all of these the woman has the ambiguous character of a dangerous and implacable, but fascinating, enemy.[98] A suggestion of this character is in fact present in the second quatrain of this sonnet. The word *furtif* is curiously disturbing, suggesting some kind of duplicity. The 'cup' from which the poet drinks recalls an incident in *L'Imagier de Harlem*, a play which is closely linked with 'Artémis' (see commentary on 'Artémis'). The hero of this play, Laurent Coster, a Faust-like figure, is being entertained by the Comte de Bloksberg, who is Satan in disguise. Bloksberg drinks to the health of Aspasie, and Coster, at his bidding, does likewise. He is fascinated by Aspasie, a beautiful, enigmatic creature who appears in many guises in this play, but is always Alilah (Lilith), Satan's slave, and the eternal betrayer of man. Coster compares the effect of drinking from the cup to being engulfed by a volcano (O.C. V, 89–90):

> Dieu! Qu'ai-je bu? . . . Quel trouble je ressens!
> Cette coupe a versé l'incendie en mes sens . . .
> La lave d'un volcan me brûle . . . Elle m'enflamme
> Comme une voix d'enfer! . . . Démon, fantôme ou femme!
> Parle: qui donc es-tu? Qui donc est-il? réponds!
> Je sens frémir sous moi les abîmes profonds . . .

The same idea is present in the next line of the sonnet, with its rather strange metaphor which speaks of the poet drinking intoxication from his lady's eye. This image is to be found in Heine's poem 'Der Schiffbrüchige' (in *Nordsee*), which Nerval translated under the title of 'Le Naufragé'.[99] Here is the passage in which Heine describes his beloved's eye and the smile on her lips:

> Dans son doux et pâle visage . . . rayonne son œil semblable à un soleil noir . . . Noir soleil, combien de fois tu m'as versé les flammes dévorantes de l'enthousiasme, et combien de fois ne suis-je pas resté chancelant sous l'ivresse de cette boisson! Mais alors un sourire d'une douceur enfantine voltigeait autour des lèvres fièrement arquées . . .

The *soleil noir* has an ambiguous quality implied in the words *flammes dévorantes* and *chancelant*, and made more terrifying by the *douceur enfantine* of the smile. The same image of the flame which attracts and then destroys occurs in Nerval's poem 'Résignation' (dated 1839; I, 38):

> Peut-être, ainsi que moi, cette fleur expirante,
> Aux ardeurs du soleil s'ouvrant avec transport,
> Enferma dans son sein la flamme dévorante
> Qui lui donna la mort.

At one point in *L'Imagier de Harlem*, Alilah appears as Impéria, filling the cups of her guests with the poisoned 'vin des Borgia'; aware of Coster's enslavement to her beauty, she remarks ambiguously: 'l'ivresse que je verse donne toujours la mort' (O.C. V, 193).

The title of Heine's poem evokes the perfidious beauty of the Sirens who lured the sailors of legend to shipwreck and death. The image of the Siren is also present in *Octavie*. In a Paris theatre, Nerval hears 'Une voix délicieuse, comme celle des sirènes . . .'; he flees to Italy to escape the danger, only to meet Octavie, 'cette fille des eaux', and the strange young woman who reminded him of 'ces magiciennes de Thessalie à qui l'on donnait son âme pour un rêve' (I, 285-9). Moreover, Posilipo, with which he associated the 'enchanteresse' of 'Myrtho', was the site of the original town of Naples, founded by Greeks from Cumae, where Aeneas found the Sibyl. The settlers called their town Parthenope, after the siren who threw herself from the cliff-top into the sea (as Nerval, in *Octavie*, is tempted to do) because of her hopeless love for Ulysses. The whole volcanic landscape is equally under the sign of the Sibyl and the Siren. In 'Delfica' it has the same duality, for the waterfalls at Tivoli (whose name accompanies 'Delfica') were crowned at the top by a little round temple known as the 'Temple de la Sibylle' (the 'sibylle Tiburtine' referred to in *Sylvie*; see commentary on 'Delfica'); and from the temple a path led down to the 'grottes de Neptune et des Sirènes' below the falls. The figure of Aspasie in *L'Imagier de Harlem* also links the image of the siren with that of fire, for a variant of the text describes her as 'naïade du Cocyte', that is, of the Cocytus, a river in Hell. She is an incarnation of Alilah, who is described by the devil as 'cette femme éternelle . . . cette syrène fatale, fille de mon souffle, esclave de ma main qui a pris tous les noms de la fable et de l'histoire pour gagner à l'Enfer tous les élus de ce monde'. Alilah the Siren is literally a *fille du feu*, daughter of the fires of Hell, 'fille de mon souffle'.[100]

It becomes obvious that there is a price to be paid for love and poetry. During his descent to the mountain's heart, Adoniram is able to breathe in the element of fire. He goes barefoot in the forge, 'car il foulait impunément le métal rougi' (II, 549), as Myrtho with her *pied agile* walks on the slopes of the volcano. Such intimacy with the element of fire is possible in myth and poetry; the reality was rather different, as Nerval ruefully acknowledged in a letter from Marseille in 1834 (I, 793): 'Naples, quand je pense que la cendre chaude du Vésuve n'a pas peu contribué à la démoralisation de mes bottes! Cela avait desséché le cuir, qui s'est fendu'. The earlier version of the first tercet, in 'à J-y Colonna', claims for the poet, as well as for the woman, the ability to bring the volcano to life; but their act of love, which has caused the eruption, has also filled the sky with ashes: 'C'est qu'un jour nous l'avions touché d'un pied agile Et de sa poudre au loin l'horizon s'est couvert!' Like the *magicienne* of *Octavie*, 'ce fantôme qui me séduisait et m'effrayait à la fois', the volcanic fires of love are potentially both life-giving and destructive, and Nerval is afraid of them, at the same time as he desires them.

Both these aspects of fire are made plain in 'Myrtho'; but the sonnet ends by asserting an eternity of harmony, none the less real for being symbolised by the intertwining of vulnerable plants. If a question remains in one's mind, it is due to the ambiguity of the *éclair furtif*; to the suggestion, implied only in the syntax of the final tercet, that the violence in the word *brisa* may be a necessary condition of the unity which follows it; and to the sense that the poet is not altogether willing to accept that necessity, nor to face the dangers of the *flammes dévorantes* in which he is reborn.

The hesitations implicit in the tercets of 'Myrtho' may explain why they were detached from the quatrains which now stand in 'Delfica'. In 1845 Nerval added to those quatrains lines which mask the intensely personal concerns we can detect in 'Myrtho'. Only by comparing 'Delfica' with 'Myrtho' and 'El Desdichado' could the reader understand the full implications of 'la grotte fatale', and that was not possible until 1854. In 'Myrtho' itself the tercets are matched with equally revealing quatrains. That may be the reason why, like 'Horus' and 'Antéros', it was not published earlier, but had to await the publication of *Les Chimères* as a whole.

The hesitations of 'Myrtho' are not unlike those already noted in 'Vers Dorés', except that the focus of the problem has shifted to a more personal—or more obviously personal—plane. Both 'Vers Dorés' and 'Delfica' make it clear that participation in the life of the world, and the possibility of rebirth, depend on love. The terms 'un mystère d'amour', 'cette chanson d'amour', neatly sum up the two sides of the problem. The word *mystère* in 'Vers Dorés' means a communion, that transcendent and timeless unity of man, nature and God which the poet describes in *Aurélia*, and which he thought of as the highest joy. The *chanson* of 'Delfica' symbolises human love, renewed with each generation, end-lessly recurring though never the same, and an image, though imperfectly so, of the *mystère d'amour*. The way to the *mystère*, as we have seen, was made difficult both by the objections of reason and intelligence, and by irrational fears of the powers of evil. The *chanson*, it now becomes clear, is equally hard to accept: it may be the song of the Siren. Despite the insistence on unity in the final verse of 'Myrtho', the existence of harmony seems, in the light of these under-currents, more wished-for than real. The poet is not yet ready to effect the reconciliation he desires.

HORUS

The first thing that strikes one about this poem (p. 45) is that the sense of distance, already growing in 'Myrtho', seems to have been sharply increased. The subject is presented in narrative form, and entirely as an event in the past, though the drama is made more vivid by the use, in the second quatrain and the first tercet, of direct speech in the present and perfect tenses. The poet himself does not obviously appear in this sonnet at all. His involvement is nonetheless certain, though it is only implied in such unobtrusive details as the word *nous* in the penultimate line, which indicates that the poet has been a witness to the events which the poem describes, and in the 'Le voyez-vous . . .' with which the goddess Isis seems to be calling his attention to what is happening.

The central figures, Kneph and Isis, are presented as actors in a domestic drama which might almost be comic if it were not related to the universe of myth. Certainly it retains a large measure of humanity in the details of physical action, which are much more numerous in this poem than in 'Delfica' or 'Myrtho': 'se leva sur sa couche', 'fit un geste de haine', 'j'ai revêtu pour lui la robe de Cybèle'; there is humanity also in the physical traits which characterise the actors: 'ses yeux verts', 'son pied tors . . . son œil louche', and in the familiarity of the goddess's speech: 'Le voyez-vous, dit-elle, il meurt, ce vieux pervers'. If a woman can be a goddess, a goddess, it seems, can also be a woman.

Yet it is evident that the events described are not significant only at the human level. The trembling of the dying god shakes the universe to its foundations, as did the death of Christ in 'Le Christ aux Oliviers'. Isis, without the slightest hesitation, abandons him for *l'esprit nouveau*, a new god who is her own child Horus—but not the son of Kneph: 'C'est l'enfant bien-aimé d'Hermès et d'Osiris'. Horus was the son of Osiris, husband of Isis, who restored Osiris to life by her love for him, after he had been murdered by Seth. Hermes, a god of the Underworld, was the spiritual father and protector of Horus. The theme of this sonnet is evidently related to the theme of the rebirth of the gods in 'Delfica', the old world being apparently rejected, in this poem, in favour of the new. This theme is of course implicit in the choice of Horus as the central, though unseen, figure in the drama: Egyptian legend sees Horus as the child who brings light from the darkness of the underworld: he is the rising sun, the returning spring, and the flooding of the Nile, yet another in the series of figures symbolising death and rebirth, an *éternelle victime* like Atys or Christ. Like them, and like Antéros, he is linked in exclusive union with his mother. Isis is here primarily *la mère*, the mother-goddess whose image fascinated Nerval at Pompeii. He describes her in *Aurélia* as 'la mère et l'épouse sacrée' (I, 404), but in relation to himself he always sees her as a maternal figure, and compares her with Cybele, the earth-mother, and with the goddess Venus (*Isis*; I, 300–3). This poem makes the same synthesis. Isis emphasises her rôle as mother by putting on 'la robe de Cybèle'; and the gilded shell which carries her away ('La déesse avait fui sur sa conque dorée . . .') is an attribute of Venus Anadyomene, and the vessel on which the sea-born Venus of Botticelli floats to the shore. Moreover, the description of Isis on her couch beside her ferocious husband recalls Vergil's description (in the Eighth Book of the *Æneid*) of Venus and her consort Vulcan. From Vulcan, the god of fire with the twisted foot, the goddess Venus begged the magic armour she gave to her son Aeneas (who was not Vulcan's son): Kneph too has a *pied tors*, and he too is *le dieu des volcans*.[101] It is worth noting that at this point the image in the poet's mind is not that of 'la Vénus austère, idéale et mystique', who is compared with 'la Vierge des chrétiens' and whom Nerval himself preferred, but of the popular Venus whom he called 'la Vénus frivole des poëtes, la mère des Amours, l'épouse légère du boiteux Vulcain'.[102] In 'Horus', something of the criticism this description implies seems to be directed at the figure of Isis, whose attitude to her dying husband, if we allow ourselves to see the situation in human terms (and we are encouraged to do so), borders on callousness.

The volcano links this poem again with 'Myrtho' and with 'Delfica', and the nature of the image in 'Horus' suggests a possible further reason for the sinister elements it seems to bring to 'Myrtho' in particular. Kneph, god of volcanoes, is a dangerous god; even though he is dying, Isis commands that his foot should be tied and his eye put out. Paradoxically, he is both god of volcanoes, and therefore of fire, and king of the winter. He is, that is to say, a volcano which seems extinct and cold, pouring out ice instead of fire: 'Tous les frimas du monde ont passé par sa bouche'. Yet he still trembles, and shakes the universe with his trembling, as the death of Christ shakes Olympus, and as the earth shakes in 'Delfica': 'La terre a tressailli d'un souffle prophétique'. Is the volcano about to come to life again, as it does in 'Myrtho'? The power of fire, it is again made clear, is potentially dangerous as well as restorative; so that the emotions the dying god arouses in Isis are not pity and love, but hatred and fear, and joy at his dying.

'Horus' gains an added dimension (which incidentally may explain the domestic drama in which the myth is embodied) when we know that Nerval's own father was lame: he was wounded three times in the left foot during the Napoleonic wars. On a personal level, the poem seems to be envisaging a situation in which the poet's mother will leave her husband to devote herself to her child. In real life, the opposite was the case, for Madame Labrunie abandoned her child to follow her husband to Silesia, where she died. Even at this level, however, the poem means more than a simple rejection of a hated father. Nerval's mother was an unknown and unknowable ideal; his father was a reality. Despite the obvious longing in this poem, as in 'Antéros', for exclusive union with the ideal mother, the god of fire is equally a source of life and power, and cannot be discounted. Even if one is unaware of the personal relevance of the image of Kneph, one can sense that the poet feels a kind of reluctant awe and admiration for the tragic figure of the dying god, which in some ways is reinforced by the strongly negative attitude of Isis to her 'époux farouche'. The image of Kneph is like that of Kronion, 'le roi du ciel', in Heine's poem 'Les Dieux grecs' (from *Nordsee*), which Nerval had translated (see note 99): 'les hivers ont neigé sur les boucles de ses cheveux, de ces cheveux célèbres qui, en s'agitant, faisaient trembler l'Olympe';[103] and there is the same feeling of awe. Heine sees in the moonlit clouds the 'spectres gigantesques' of the ancient gods, and though he cannot love them, he pities them:

> une sainte pitié et une ardente compassion s'emparent de mon cœur, lorsque je vous vois là-haut, dieux abandonnés, ombres mortes et errantes . . . Il est vrai qu'autrefois, vieux dieux, vous avez toujours, dans les batailles des hommes, pris le parti des vainqueurs; mais l'homme a l'âme plus généreuse que vous, et, dans les combats des dieux, moi, je prends le parti des dieux vaincus.

Moreover, as 'le dieu des volcans' the god Kneph has possessed—and perhaps still governs—the life-giving fire which enabled the poet of 'Myrtho' to re-establish his links with both faith and poetry. He is thus an ambiguous figure, both envied and disliked, admired and greatly feared. The artist Adoniram is afraid of the fire of the forge, which he must use to cast the bronzes for the Temple of Soliman; he is even more afraid to enter the inner fires of earth. His ancestor Tubal-Kain reassures him: 'quand ma main aura glissé sur ton front, tu respireras dans la flamme' (*Voyage en Orient*; II, 556). Adoniram's guide, who describes himself as 'l'ombre du père de tes pères', can dominate the power of fire; Adoniram can do the same, and assume the power of his fathers, but first he must conquer his fear, and Tubal-Kain repeatedly bids him 'Sois sans crainte'. This fear is a fear that one may be unequal to the task, that the power of fire may be beyond one's strength to control, that one may be burned. The fear of one's own weakness is naturally accompanied by fear of the superior power which can apparently govern fire; but even that is not a simple emotion: the mixture of feelings with which Kneph is regarded in 'Horus' is recognised by Adoniram as part of the essence of love: 'On ne craint . . . que ce que l'on aime' (Ibid.; II, 577).

The fact that the poet cannot adopt a unified attitude to the fire-god no doubt explains the distance he keeps between himself and the events which he describes. Since he is uncertain of his feelings, hatred for the god is attributed solely to Isis, who seems to be trying to justify her attitude in the eyes of the poet-spectator. Such uncertainty may also explain why this poem, like 'Myrtho', ends in an evasion—in this case literally: 'La déesse avait fui . . .' The final tercet offers us a brilliant image of gilded shell on sparkling water, under the rainbow (*l'écharpe d'Iris*) which is a perennial symbol of hope,[104] and of the reconciliation of men and gods (and as such it appears briefly in 'Le Christ aux Oliviers'). But the poet turns abruptly to this vision as Isis ceases speaking, and there is a curious hiatus between the two tercets, as if he were changing the subject. The goddess's flight may thus symbolise the inability of the poet himself to face and resolve his conflicting emotions; and that conflict is doubtless responsible for the hesitant evolution of this sonnet, and for its delayed publication.

An earlier version of 'Horus' appears on a manuscript in the Dumesnil de Gramont collection; it is on the same sheet as five other sonnets, including 'à Madame Aguado' and 'à J-y Colonna' (which are related to 'Delfica' and 'Myrtho'), and bears the title 'à Louise d'Or Reine'. A number of important variants occur in that version (reproduced in note 105), and they are not merely variants of stylistic detail, or, as with some of the alternative readings of 'Delfica', musical roughnesses which were later smoothed out. In the first line, the name of Kneph does not appear; the line reads: 'Le *vieux père* en tremblant ébranlait l'univers ...'; in the fifth line, the words *il meurt* are replaced by *il dort*; and in the seventh line 'Attachez son pied tors' appears as 'Prenez garde à son pied'. In 'Horus', Isis is impelled to follow *l'esprit nouveau*; the earlier version of the first tercet evokes a more precise set of connotations: 'L'aigle a déjà passé: Napoléon m'appelle';[106] and no reference is made to a child in the eleventh line, which reads 'C'est mon époux Hermès, et mon frère Osiris'. The changes made to this version are interesting, for they seem to follow a pattern. The first version is centred on the figure of 'Isis la mère', and while the *geste de haine* is already there, the portrait of 'Le vieux père' is curiously guarded in comparison with the later version. Although he is described as *père*, his child is nowhere mentioned; and we are less likely, in reading this version, to make the identification with the god Vulcan: his foot is not described as twisted, and as if further to conceal his identity, his titles are reversed: 'C'est le roi des volcans et le Dieu des hivers'. In the earlier image of an old man sleeping, there is little of the tragic feeling and half-reluctant awe which the dying god of 'Horus' inspires; perhaps because of this, the words of Isis seem milder and less dramatic. The goddess does not order her husband's foot to be tied, but only asks us to beware of it, or perhaps simply to notice it: the words 'Prenez garde à son pied' might mean either, or both. But is this because she is less afraid of him, or because she is less ready to defy him? The poet's own attitude to the situation is even less clear in 'à Louise d'Or Reine' than it is in 'Horus'. Later, the removal of the reference to Napoleon removes the whole sonnet from the sphere of contemporary action to the timeless world of mythology, giving to the personal references the same universal significance that the links with mythology give to the experience in 'Delfica'. At the same time, Isis names the new spirit unequivocally as her own child, and the 'vieux père' becomes 'le dieu Kneph', whose relationship with that child is denied. The notion that Isis's child was not the son of her husband Kneph, as Aeneas was not the son of Vulcan, reflects a wish to be rid of the frightening father. Nerval is known to have entertained a fantasy of a similar kind in his own case; Alexandre Weill records[107] that in a moment of manic elation Nerval once assured him that he was the natural son of Joseph Bonaparte (and thus related to Napoleon, for whom Isis left 'le vieux père' in the earlier version of this sonnet). If the poet is tempted to deny his links with his father, it is obviously because he would like to avoid the necessity of maintaining the interchange of love with a difficult deity, of succeeding, that is, where the race of Cain had failed (see commentary on 'Myrtho', p. 88). But like the dream of reunion with the ideal mother, rejection of father or god is a poetic possibility only. Even in the sonnet, the goddess's departure leaves the poet with a companion ('La mer *nous* renvoyait . . .') who must surely be Kneph, so that he has still to face the problem of his own attitude to the god. In his own life, Nerval never abandoned the attempt to maintain his links with his father, however little encouragement he received. His nostalgia for a loving father was as important a part of his emotional life as his dream of a loving mother. Even Adoniram, 'fils du feu', is moved by the nearness of his father's spirit (*Voyage en Orient*; II, 566):

'. . . ton père, Adoniram, est errant dans l'air enflammé que tu respires . . . Oui, ton père.

—Ton père, oui, ton père . . .', redit comme un écho, mais avec un accent tendre, une voix qui passa comme un baiser sur le front d'Adoniram.

Et se retournant l'artiste pleura.

The changes we have observed in the text suggest that the poet was feeling his way, over a period of time, towards a full realisation of the poem's theme; and it seems likely that the earlier version, whether consciously or not, obscures a reference to the poet's personal situation which by 1854 he was more able to accept, or more willing to reveal. But one can sense a conflict in the dramatic form of the sonnet even without knowing the personal relevance of the images for Nerval. The presence of conflict makes it less surprising that the final tercet of this poem, like that of 'Delfica', should offer no certainties, but only the promise of better things. The sleeping Sibyl can be seen as a hope for the future only if the poet has faith in the power of the 'chanson d'amour' to restore the vanished gods. The hope in itself is as fragile as the intertwined plants of 'Myrtho', as evanescent as the rainbow: and the goddess in 'Horus' is moving *away from* the poet, leaving him only her *image adorée* as proof of her existence.

The word *adorée* suggests that the poet has been charged with the task of maintaining the life of the goddess by continuing to adore her, even when she has left him; and conversely, Kneph is dying *because* the goddess does not love him. This idea links 'Horus' with the third sonnet of 'Le Christ aux Oliviers', in which the effective existence of God appears to depend on Christ's continuing belief that God is within him. In the same

way, the return of the ancient gods in 'Delfica' may depend on the fact
that Dafné still weeps for them :'Ils reviendront ces dieux que tu pleures
toujours!' The idea is made explicit in *Voyage en Orient* (II, 1292, n.9):
'Ainsi les dieux s'éteignent eux-mêmes, ou quittent la terre, vers qui
l'amour des hommes ne les appelle plus! Leurs bocages ont été coupés,
leurs sources taries, leurs sanctuaires profanés; par où leur serait-il
possible de se manifester encore?' And again: ' "Pan est mort!" ' . . . mort
comme un dieu peut seulement mourir, faute d'encens et d'hommages,
et frappé au cœur comme un père par l'ingratitude et l'oubli!' (II, 87).
Only the continuing love of men can save the gods from oblivion, just
as only the continuing love of those who loved them in life, can save the
dead from total destruction; Nerval particularly notes in his Preface to
Faust (1840) that Goethe postulates the existence of a region in space
where the spirits of the dead can float for ever, 'protégées contre le néant
par la puissance du souvenir' (O.C. I, 18). It is a theme which plays its
part in 'Artémis'. The continuance of life depends on love. Paradoxically,
although 'Horus' appears to be centred around a 'geste de haine', it
finally makes abundantly clear the necessity of love, and the consequences
of its failure.

ANTÉROS

No other versions of 'Antéros' (p. 46) are known to exist, either in
manuscript form or in print; it appears to have been published for the
first time in 1854 in *Les Filles du Feu*. It may therefore be later in date of
composition than 'Delfica', 'Myrtho' and 'Horus', of which earlier
manuscript versions do exist; but we have no way of knowing. The
greater allusiveness of its style also suggests that it may belong to a
somewhat later period.

This sonnet does not present us with figures in a landscape, as 'Delfica',
'Myrtho' and 'Horus' do. Names of men and gods appear, but no mention
is made of particular incidents, nor are these figures described with the
sort of vivid human detail that makes Dafné, Myrtho or Isis come alive
for us. These men and gods are not important for their own sakes, but
only in so far as they help to define the nature of the speaker, who *is* Abel,
Cain, Anteus and the son of the Amalekite woman, and who confronts
the remote and victorious god Jehovah as his ancestors Baal and Dagon
did before him. So tight is the construction of the poem that the emotion
aroused by each of these names is determined by the sonnet itself, and
not by any previous significance they may have had for the reader.
Typical of this effect are the seventh and eighth lines:

> Sous la pâleur d'Abel, hélas! ensanglantée,
> J'ai parfois de Caïn l'implacable rougeur!

The emphasis in these lines is not on the conventional contrast between pathetic victim, pale and streaked with blood, and the implacable murderer, flushed with anger. It is not even certain that it is Cain who is *implacable*; the adjective belongs to *rougeur*, and seems to signify the impossibility of escaping from the destiny symbolised by the mark of Cain. There is in any case no question of a true opposition: the speaker is both Cain and Abel. The rhythm of the lines places the vocal stress on the two names, each situated just before the caesura at the sixth syllable, each forming the central point of a classically balanced alexandrine. The distance from Abel to Cain is lessened by the parenthetical 'hélas! ensanglantée', which gives to the seventh line a sighing, fading close; the eighth line follows with the force of contrast, the sounds firm and deliberate, moving towards the climax at the hemistich: 'J'ai parfois de Caïn . . . l'implacable rougeur!' The total effect is not pictorial but symbolic; one feels a comparison between Abel and Cain, between yielding softness and firm resistance, suggested in the sound of the words. The names do not evoke particular human beings, but fundamental attitudes and the destinies they entail.

The general tone of the sonnet is one of defiance, and for most of its length it has a driving energy and an apparently unshaken conviction which is quite unlike the reflective tone of 'Myrtho' or the hesitations of 'Delfica' and 'Horus'. It is intensely dramatic, for there is no scene-setting and no stage directions; the words are spoken directly, and we know no more of the speaker than what he says of himself. His words are addressed to someone whose identity we cannot know, but who seems to be ourselves, so immediate is the voice in our ears: 'Tu demandes pourquoi j'ai tant de rage au cœur . . .'

The defiance this sonnet expresses is that of a spirit overcome by a brute force whose moral superiority it nevertheless refuses to admit. In this the speaker resembles the Lucifer of Byron's *Cain*, of which a translation by Fabre d'Olivet appeared in 1823. The French Romantic poets greatly admired Byron, whom they regarded as a demonic figure somewhat akin to Lucifer himself—their image of Lucifer being determined by Milton's heroic portrait of the dark angel in *Paradise Lost*. Nerval mentions both Byron's verse-play and Fabre d'Olivet in his essay on Bouton's Diorama (II, 1234; see commentary on 'Le Christ aux Oliviers' and note 63). Byron's Lucifer denies the moral victory of God; in Fabre d'Olivet's translation: 'Il est mon vainqueur, oui; mais mon supérieur, non'. The speaker in 'Antéros' considers himself to be a child of the race of Cain, who was himself, according to ancient tradition, the child of the Serpent who tempted Eve (see commentary on 'Delfica', pp. 77-8). The children of Cain are condemned for all time to work for the children of Adonai (or Jehovah); but they know their own superior worth. In *Voyage en Orient*, the son of Tubal-Kain tells Adoniram of the destiny which Adonai decreed for the children of Cain (II, 567):

'Souche de géants, j'ai humilié ton corps; tes descendants naîtront faibles; leur vie sera courte; l'isolement sera leur partage . . . Supérieurs aux hommes, ils en seront les bienfaiteurs et se verront l'objet de leurs dédains . . . Soumis à des pouvoirs médiocres et vils, ils échoueront à surmonter ces tyrans méprisables . . . Géants de l'intelligence, flambeaux du savoir, organes du progrès, lumières des arts, instruments de la liberté, eux seuls resteront esclaves, dédaignés, solitaires. . .'

Jéhovah dit; mon cœur fut brisé . . .

There is no doubt that the hero of this sonnet has been defeated: his enemy is described as 'le dieu *vainqueur*'; but though his physical appearance is one of submission ('un col flexible . . . la pâleur d'Abel'), his heart and mind remain unconquered, and he does not admit the justice of his subjection. It should be noted, however, that the rebellion is a silent one: it is not the 'Je' of the sonnet who cries 'O tyrannie!', but his forebears. He himself has 'tant de rage *au cœur*', 'une *tête* indomptée', and sometimes the 'implacable rougeur' of Cain; but it is hidden beneath the pallor of Abel.

The sonnet begins by offering an answer to someone who has asked why the poet is angry and defiant. He replies that it is because he belongs to 'la race d'Antée'. The implication is that he has no real choice in the matter, but is destined by birth to refuse the authority of 'le dieu vainqueur'. The giant Antaeus was a son of the earth-goddess Gaea and the sea-god Poseidon, and thus opposed to the sky-god Zeus: like Atys, the son of Cybele, he drew his strength from his mother the earth. When Hercules wrestled with Antaeus, he was unable to defeat the giant by throwing him to the ground, for every contact with the earth gave Antaeus new strength; Hercules finally overcame him by lifting him into the air. In *Angélique*, Nerval describes his return to the Valois, the home of his mother's family, as a rebirth like that of Antaeus: 'je reprends des forces sur cette terre maternelle' (I, 189). The speaker in 'Antéros' seems thus to imply that he too draws from his mother the strength to defy the victorious god who rules him.

The second quatrain moves from classical mythology to Biblical sources, from Jupiter to Jehovah; it evokes the anger of Cain, the murder of Abel, and the sign with which God marked Cain. We scarcely have time to consider the significance of these references, for the poem sweeps onward to the first tercet with a loud cry of defiance: 'Jéhovah!' The victorious god is reminded that his victim is descended from Bélus (Baal) and Dagon, both pagan gods whose ascendancy had been overthrown by the cult of Jehovah, and who, we are told, had proclaimed aloud the tyranny of their conqueror. Nerval links Bélus with Apollo: 'Baal le Dieu Soleil' (*Carnet de Notes du Voyage en Orient*; II, 717), and this sonnet evidently refers to the same pattern of the rise and fall of the gods that we have seen in 'Le Christ aux Oliviers', 'Delfica' and 'Horus': it is suggested that Jehovah will be defeated in his turn. The mood of 'Antéros' is different, however. It provides a counterpart to the third sonnet of 'Le Christ aux Oliviers'. The overthrow of God, which Christ had feared, is here desired. The 'ange des nuits', who is Lucifer, Cain and Antéros, is exalted as a power more human and more noble than God.

The rebelliousness which rejects God in order to exalt the semi-divine nature of man is a basic human attitude, to be found in the earliest myths; it is an attitude of whose limitations Nerval was aware. The value of intelligence alone is doubted in 'Vers Dorés'. In his article on Bouton's Diorama (which influenced also 'Le Christ aux Oliviers') Nerval describes how 'la lutte des esprits rebelles contre le Tout-Puissant' led to a tremendous development of man's power over nature. The Flood was God's answer to these 'demi-dieux' (II, 1235): 'C'est à ce point juste où l'homme se fait Dieu par son adresse et par son industrie, que Dieu l'arrête et lui démontre qu'on ne doit s'élever à lui que par l'esprit et par l'amour'. It is the lesson which Icarus and Phaeton also had to learn. It is the real sense of the myth of Prometheus, whom Antéros so much resembles (see Introduction).

The pattern of this sonnet is like that of 'Delfica', 'Myrtho' and 'Horus'; it develops a single line of argument, with mounting conviction, until the end of the first tercet, where like them it suddenly breaks off. The final tercet of 'Antéros' unexpectedly appears to turn away from defiance. The last three lines are extremely compressed in comparison with the flowing movement of the quatrains and the first tercet. The speaker returns to himself, and states without comment that 'they' (whom he does not identify) have plunged him three times into the waters of the Cocytus. This river, whose name means 'lamentation', was a tributary of the Acheron, and believed by the Greeks to flow down into the Under-world. Is the poet referring to a punishment, or to an initiation or purification rite? The latter seems more likely, since immersion in underground waters was part of the initiation ceremonies of the cults of Isis which Nerval describes in *Voyage en Orient* (II, 226). Moreover, this verse is linked with the following verses by the simple conjunction *Et*; that is, it appears to be the first step in a series of quietly positive actions which are placed in apparent opposition to the frustrated anger of the quatrains. It seems as if the poet is saying 'I may not cry "O tyranny!" as my forebears did, but I have my own solution to offer'. That solution links 'Antéros' at once with 'Horus'. The exclusive relationship with the mother is here shown from the point of view of the child. She is 'ma mère Amalécyte', and therefore a descendant of Esau, who, like Cain, saw his brother preferred and lost his birthright. In this she resembles her child, who likens himself to Cain. Mother and child in this poem are like the poet and the girl in 'Delfica': they are *déshérités*. The speaker claims the exclusive right to defend his mother against her enemies: 'protégeant tout seul ma mère Amalécyte . . .'; the implication is clearly that she needs no one else to defend her; mother and child are safe if they cling to each other.

The final line introduces an idea of renewal ('je ressème') which links the poem with 'Delfica', in which the dragon's seed symbolises the sleeping gods who await rebirth, and the race of Cain who will one day reinherit the earth (see commentary on 'Delfica', pp. 77–9). The sowing of the dragon's teeth again suggests that the power of man's reason is his strongest weapon against tyranny, even the tyranny of God: in *Aurélia*, the dreamer in his despair likewise refuses to submit: 'luttons contre le dieu lui-même avec les armes de la tradition et de la science' (I, 382). Nerval uses the image of the dragon's teeth in his play *Léo Burckart* (1839; Scene X): 'Vous philosophe, vous écrivain, vous avez ouvert une porte à la guerre et une autre à la révolte . . . vous savez qu'il y a des paroles qui tuent, et que, grâce à la presse, l'intelligence marche aujourd'hui sur la terre, comme ce héros antique qui semait les dents du dragon!' (see note 85). Intelligence and self-assertion are not abandoned altogether; but since they are not in themselves enough, since the road to God is not only 'par l'esprit' but also 'par l'amour' (see p. 100), 'Antéros' links the idea of renewal with the idea of love, as in 'Delfica' and 'Myrtho': the hero's sowing of the dragon's seed is made as an offering to his mother: 'je ressème *à ses pieds*'.

It is important to note that although the final tercet substitutes constructive action and love for rebellion and anger, it does not altogether abandon the defiance expressed in the earlier part of the sonnet. The words 'protégeant tout seul ma mère' pick up the idea implicit in the image of Antaeus, son of the earth-mother. As in 'Horus', God-the-father is rejected. But the speaker seems to have chosen to avoid the open defiance of Baal and Dagon, in favour of the patient vigil of Cain; he makes the gesture of hope and faith which is the sowing of seed, and asserts the positive values of patience and love as opposed to the negative force of hatred. Indeed, a closer look at the earlier part of the sonnet reveals that even there, there is no true expression of hatred. Antéros, like Eros, was a son of Venus, and according to the myth, his task was that of avenging unrequited love. The figure of 'le Vengeur' is thus not that of an indiscriminate rebel, but quite specifically that of a god who punishes those who do not love in return when love is offered to them.

Hence the choice of the images of Cain and Abel: Cain was jealous of Abel, whom God preferred, and angrily disappointed because his offering of love had been refused while his brother's was accepted. In *Voyage en Orient* (II, 561), Cain talks to Adoniram about his parents, Adam and Eve. It is plain that he was hurt by the ingratitude with which they accepted his skill and effort in making a new Eden of their land of exile; but he was clearly much more hurt by the fact that neither of them loved him: they, like God, preferred Abel. The defiance of this sonnet is not born of hatred, or even of true rejection. It is the angry defiance of a disappointed child who feels he is not loved, and who would like in return to withdraw his own affection and assert his independence. The complex emotions attached to the image of Jehovah in 'Antéros' are similar, in fact, to those attached to the god Kneph in 'Horus', and these two sonnets illuminate each other. There are further hints of this conflict in the exchanges between Adoniram and Soliman in the *Voyage en Orient*, in Nerval's letters to his father, and in a passage of *Aurélia* where Nerval speaks of the difficulty of accepting without question the absolute authority of God the Father.[108] Persevering in love for God or father (for the two are evidently one) is difficult, and the poet is often tempted to abandon the struggle, either by denying his links with the father-god, as in 'Horus', or by defying him, as in 'Antéros'. But whatever the difficulties, one must continue to love and trust, for the free exchange of warm affection is the only way, as Cain tells Adoniram, to achieve 'la vie sans fin'. Despite its images of conflict, 'Antéros' does conclude with an affirmation of love; but it is here a love of an exclusive and embattled kind, limited to a chosen object, intense but deliberately narrow in scope.

The tenses of the verbs in this sonnet emphasise the constant presence of the emotions it sets out to define. The only real past tense is *cria*, which refers to the actions not of the speaker but of his ancestors; and even they are thought of as still living in their exile in hell: 'C'*est* mon aieul Bélus ou mon père Dagon'. Thus the 'j'ai tant de rage au cœur' of the first quatrain is contemporaneous with the 'je ressème' of the final verse; the speaker's efforts to assert a positive value through devotion to his mother and work for the future, do not cancel the 'rage' with which he begins: the one is in fact the cause of the other, and must exist alongside it. Exclusive love for the mother is a refuge against the overwhelming destiny which opposes him to the god, and it is a love which is forced constantly to defend itself. There is thus no hint in 'Antéros' of the kind of general reconciliation that is envisaged in 'Myrtho', and finally achieved in *Aurélia*. This sonnet arrives at only a partial resolution of its problems, and its angry despair seems to indicate that the poet is aware of the fact.

ARTÉMIS

This sonnet (p. 48) was first published in *Les Filles du Feu* (1854);
another version is to be found on the manuscript which belonged to
Paul Eluard, where it accompanies 'Erythréa' (see commentary on 'Del-
fica') and a version of 'El Desdichado' which bears the title 'Le Destin'.
It appears also, again with 'El Desdichado', on the manuscript sold to
M. Alfred Lombard in 1935, where its title is given as 'Ballet des Heures'.[109]

'Artémis' appears at first sight to lack the formal cohesion which can
be observed in the rest of the sonnets; it is without doubt the most
difficult of access. This makes one wonder whether in fact we are inten-
ded to find a 'way in' to this sonnet. The present writer's own experience
of it is that any attempt at paraphrase or explanation invariably dis-
locates its structure to such an extent that one is left with a handful of
apparently meaningless fragments. On the other hand, if the sonnet is
read aloud without pause, it has an obvious unity at least of mood and
feeling; one can sense a meaning in its whole, but it is a meaning which
seems to vanish as soon as one tries to break it down into its parts. It
seems likely that the real difficulty of this sonnet is not that it lacks
cohesion, but that it is *all* cohesion, an indivisible structure which is not
made according to the normal patterns of discursive speech. Jean
Richer has called this poem a 'tombeau' (that is, a memorial poem).[110]
Certainly one has the impression of confronting a monument, and a
sense of enclosed and forbidden space. Of all Nerval's poems, this is the
one which most nearly shuts us out.

The first quatrain begins with a statement:

La Treizième revient . . . C'est encor la première;

Et c'est toujours la seule,—ou c'est le seul moment:

The Eluard manuscript has a note against the first line: 'La XIIIe
heure (pivotale)'; that is, the thirteenth hour in a time-scale of twenty-
four hours, which is the same as 'la première', the first hour after noon.
The alternative title 'Ballet des Heures' supports this interpretation. How-
ever, even if we did not have the manuscripts, the quatrain itself makes
it perfectly clear that some kind of eternal round is being contemplated:
'La Treizième *revient*'—it has evidently been here before: 'C'est encor la
première'—another cycle is beginning; and since the end is the same as
the beginning (the thirteenth is also the first), the cycle must be one
that is constant and never-ending.

The second line at once appears to contradict the idea of a succession
or sequence: 'c'est toujours la seule'; there is only one, whether it be
first or last. But the conjunction *Et* does not imply contradiction. The
definition it introduces must be added to what has gone before. Whatever
is first and last is *also* always the same: 'le seul', or 'la seule', is not, in *Les*

Chimères, an epithet defining solitude, but an assertion of uniqueness of kind,[111] and thus equivalent here to 'le même', 'la même'. The word *toujours*, which contains the idea of things existing in the dimension of time, explains how a sequence can also be a single, unique figure: the succession is a series in time, and it is one in which all the terms are identical: 'C'est toujours la seule'. It follows that when once we know one element in this series, we know them all. Moreover, if all are the same, any one of them could be the first or last. It does not matter then at what point in time the poet's consciousness intersects with the continuum, the result will be the same; thus all points are 'pivotal': 'ou c'est le seul moment'. The whole series can be known in any one of its terms, and the whole of time is summed up in any single moment.

To the reader, this notion of a 'seul moment' seems to offer a point of stillness in the ever-moving circle. But like the colon with which the poet ends this second line, it offers only a temporary stillness. Like the moment of certainty in 'Delfica', it cannot last, for the continuous round is apparently eternal, and we are allowed only an illusion of rest. Our apprehension of time is entirely subjective, as Nerval remarked long before Bergson and Proust: 'Il y a des moments où la vie multiple ses pulsations en dépit des lois du temps, comme une horloge folle dont la chaîne est brisée; d'autres où tout se traîne en sensations inappréciables ou peu dignes d'être notées' (*Voyage en Orient*; II, 425). The image of the runaway clock obsessed him. It appears notably in his Preface of 1840 to Goethe's *Faust*, a preface in which many of Nerval's *idées maîtresses* are to be found; he speaks of Faust's heroic flight 'hors du temps', which seemed to Nerval a journey to the spheres where lost loves still exist (O.C. I, 20–1):

> Le cercle d'un siècle vient donc de recommencer, l'action se fixe et se précise; mais, à partir du débarquement d'Hélène, elle va franchir les temps avec la rapidité du rêve . . . l'horloge éternelle, retardée par un doigt invisible, et fixée de nouveau à un certain jour passé depuis longtemps, va se détraquer, comme un mouvement dont la chaîne est brisée, et marquer ensuite peut-être un siècle pour chaque heure.

In the preface to *Les Filles du Feu* (I, 151), he uses the same image to describe his own imaginative flight through time: 'Du moment que j'avais cru saisir la série de toutes mes existences antérieures, il ne m'en coûtait pas plus d'avoir été prince, roi, mage, génie et même Dieu, la chaîne était brisée et marquait les heures pour des minutes'. The imagination is what controls one's apprehension of time, and one can live many lives in the space of time that is measured by mechanical clocks. In Byron's *Cain*, Lucifer shows Cain the panorama of the worlds in space; Cain, returning to his wife Adah, believes he has been travelling through the universe for years, and is amazed when she tells him that he has been

away only two hours. Cain realises that his sorrow has lengthened time
(Fabre d'Olivet's translation):

> Ainsi donc notre esprit
> Est le maître du temps; et selon qu'il jouit
> Ou qu'il souffre, l'allonge ou bien le raccourcit!

The only way to escape from this world of illusions (if one wanted to
escape) would be to stop time altogether. Yet the poet can imitate
Faust's flight 'hors du temps' in some measure, by choosing to accept
the illusion and learning to use it for his own artistic purpose. In *Sylvie*
he does so by deliberately dislocating one's sense of time, superimposing
one period of the action upon another until the element of time has
ceased to be perceptible to the reader at all. The story, as he begins his
journey into the Valois (that is, into his childhood, and thus into past
time), is placed under the sign of a stopped clock; and the poet has no
watch (I, 247-8):

Quelle heure est-il?

Je n'avais pas de montre.

Au milieu de toutes les splendeurs de bric-à-brac qu'il était d'usage
de réunir à cette époque pour restaurer dans sa couleur locale un
appartement d'autrefois, brillait d'un éclat rafraîchi une de ces
pendules d'écaille de la Renaissance dont le dôme doré surmonté de la
figure du Temps est supporté par des cariatides de style médicis,
reposant à leur tour sur des chevaux à demi cabrés. La Diane his-
torique, accoudée sur son cerf, est en bas-relief sous le cadran, où
s'étalent sur un fond niellé les chiffres émaillés des heures. Le mouve-
ment, excellent sans doute, n'avait pas été remonté depuis deux
siècles.—Ce n'était pas pour savoir l'heure que j'avais acheté cette
pendule en Touraine.

Diana's clock gave the poet the illusion that time could stand still, that
two centuries had not passed, and that he was still 'sous Louis Treize',
as he says in 'Fantaisie' (I, 18):[112] 'De deux cents ans mon âme rajeunit'.
But in 'Artémis' (another name for the goddess Diana), there seems to be
no hope of escaping 'hors du temps'; for what seems to be the 'seul
moment' is not one but many, and the movement never stops.

The first quatrain continues with two questions which seem parallel;
and being linked to the first two lines by the conjunction *car*, they seem
to comment on the sonnet's initial statement, to offer evidence that what
has been said is true. These questions do not seem to expect an answer:

> Car es-tu reine, o toi! la première ou dernière?
>
> Es-tu roi, toi le seul ou le dernier amant? . . .

The only possible answer appears to be 'one cannot tell'; and this is
surely the right answer, confirming the statement of the first two lines:
all the terms in the series are alike, and are one, so that the queen must

be both first and last, the king both the only lover and the last of a long line. Nevertheless, something has been added to the initial statement. From a general consideration of time, the poem has moved to a particular instance of human experience in time, and the two symbolic figures are seen to be subject to the same laws as the hours themselves. The meeting of these two figures, implied in the word *amant*, provides a point of conjunction, like that of two planets whose orbits bring them together; it offers us again the illusion that time has been arrested, and resolved in a single moment. In *Voyage en Orient*, Nerval refers to a favourite text, the *Songe de Polyphile*, in which Francesco Colonna tells the story of the platonic love of Polyphile and Polia. They could not marry because of the difference in their social positions, and they chose to live apart 'pour être unis après la mort'. Nerval describes their escape in dreams to a pre-Christian world ruled by the goddess Venus-Urania (goddess of chaste and mystical love); he compares them to Faust (II, 73): 'ils franchissaient dans leur double rêve l'immensité de l'espace et des temps'. Love, it seems, can conquer time.

But the poet knows that the flight of love 'hors du temps' is only an illusion. In a play which Nerval wrote in collaboration with Joseph Méry, *L'Imagier de Harlem* (1851), the hero is entertained with a 'Ballet des Heures' (which was, it will be remembered, the alternative title of 'Artémis'). The enchantress Alilah summons for him the hours which are to be consumed in love—and calls them, moreover, with the rhymes of this quatrain (O.C. V, 140):

> . . . que, dans ton extase et ton bonheur d'amant,
> Chaque siècle pour toi passe comme un moment.

It seems to Laurent Coster that the Ballet is over in a moment, and he cannot believe that twelve hours can really have passed. When he tries to leave Alilah, the god Pan tells him that it is too late to go back to the world outside, for the figures in the Ballet were not hours at all, but years. Alilah explains that time is not measured in her magic world (O.C. V, 143):

> Ah! Coster, que nous font les heures?
> N'avons-nous pas l'éternité?

Cain found that grief made the hours seem long. Love is one of the things that seem to make time stand still; in consequence it flies all the faster. Coster is horrified to think that so many hours have been lost: 'Quoi! tout ce temps de fièvre et d'oubli! . . .'; he is quite unable to grasp that he has really lost twelve years. Love cannot halt the movement of time; it can only allow us to forget time for a moment.

It should be noted that the punctuation of the third and fourth lines allows a quite different, though related, reading. They could mean: 'Are you, whether you be first or last, a queen? and you, the only or the final lover, are you a king?'. It is also possible to construe the first line according to our original reading, and the second in this second way, or vice versa. Since the questions remain unanswered, and unanswerable, we cannot even be certain which questions are being asked. The richness of this poem derives indeed in large part from the fact that it poses alternatives and does not choose between them, implying through its assertions of identity and co-existence that one cannot, and need not, choose. Queen or not queen, first or last, the beloved is always one and the same, and her lover has the same unchanging nature. The word *ou* does not imply 'this object instead of that', but only that the same object has another aspect and may be seen from a different point of view. Thus on the Eluard manuscript the second line of 'Artémis' reads not 'ou c'est le seul moment', but 'Et c'est toujours la Seule et c'est le seul moment'. Clearly, *ou* and *et* are interchangeable, and to say of a thing that 'it is this or that' is the same as saying 'it is this and that'. This seems paradoxical, but if the dimension of time is added to the argument, the paradox disappears. An object appears to us at a point in time. When that point has passed, we have changed, and we look at the object with different eyes. It may or may not itself have changed; in either case it will appear to us to be different. Yet despite the multiplicity of what we apprehend from moment to moment, there is an essential reality which is always the same. This is true of time itself, which we find it hard to grasp; and equally true of the stuff of human experience, which we think we grasp when we see its multiplicity. In 'Artémis', the poet is concerned to show us its underlying unity. Just as the passing of the hours is an illusion subject to our state of mind, so the diversity of love is illusory too. One is reminded of the note in the *Carnet de Notes du Voyage en Orient* (II, 706): 'Poursuivre les mêmes traits dans des femmes diverses. Amoureux d'un type éternel';[113] and of the revelation brought to the sleeping poet by the goddess Isis (*Aurélia*; I, 399): 'Je suis la même que Marie, la même que ta mère, la même aussi que sous toutes les formes tu as toujours aimée'. The words *type éternel* in the *Carnet* refer to an ideal image of the beloved, which is removed altogether from human time; the word *toujours* in *Aurélia* underlines the repetitive, fragmentary experience of time, and of love, which is all that man can normally achieve.

The final word of the fourth line, *amant*, is picked up in the second quatrain, which begins with the one unambiguous word in the sonnet, the imperative 'Aimez'. Love is here directed towards 'qui vous aima du berceau dans la bière'. The construction is again curiously rich in meaning. One's first thought, on seeing the word *berceau*, is that the line must refer to the poet's mother (if he is addressing himself, that is; but there is also the possibility that this verse is addressed to someone else, or to everyone). If the poet's dead mother is indeed meant, one assumes that the line means 'from my cradle to her grave'. That would be a possible construction to place upon this syntax; but one cannot help accepting also the more obvious (and less restricted) meaning, 'from my cradle to *my* grave'. Unwilling to abandon love, the poet has moved from the idea of the repetition of identical loves in time, to the concept of a love which transcends human time; he is imagining lovers united after death, like Polyphile and Polia. This notion immediately suggests another possible point of stillness in the endless round: death. The poem is clearly contemplating not only the past death of the beloved, but also the inevitability of the poet's own death. But again, the possibility of rest may be an illusion: for death cannot be a genuine halt if the poet believes in the immortality of the soul:

> Celle que j'aimai seul m'aime encor tendrement:
>
> C'est la mort—ou la morte . . .

The beloved is dead—or death itself: the dead are all one, like the living: and death seems to be equated here with 'she who is dead' (*la morte*), tempting the poet with the hope of reunion in death with his love. Though she be dead, her love for the poet is still alive ('m'aime *encor*'), so that in one sense she herself is still alive: 'la rose qu'elle *tient*' brings us back to the present, as does 'm'*aime* encor'. Is the lady with the rose, 'celle que j'aimai seul', the same as 'qui vous aima', and the same as 'la reine'? or is she another, the latest in the endless succession of regal figures that revolves around the poet in the centre? The phrase 'celle que j'aimai seul' links the poem with 'Antéros': 'protégeant tout seul ma mère Amalécyte', and reinforces one's sense that 'la morte' is the poet's mother. But then, 'Je suis la même que Marie, la même que ta mère . . .'; again, we are faced with the endless recurrence of a single figure; and with the rapid alternations of the seventh line, a hint of nightmare begins to creep into the poem. There may well be a sense of desperation in the poet's contemplation of endless alternatives: she may or may not be a queen, he may or may not be her only lover, or her last; what draws him may be the memory of a dead woman, or it may be death itself. Is the poet trapped in the continuous round, unable either to get out or to find certainty within it?

By imagining the field of human experience continuing beyond the bound of death, the poet of 'Artémis' has stretched out to all eternity the uncertainties of human life. He has not answered the questions with which this sonnet begins: he has only succeeded in extending their scope. The ceaseless, inexplicable round will not end even with death, and he finds little consolation in the notion that he can be linked in love even with a disembodied spirit (and even, it appears, when he himself is dead). There is no such thing as an unalloyed happiness. His cry 'O délice! ô tourment!' shows that he finds both joy and terror in the idea of an eternal love, co-extensive with eternal time. This need not surprise us. For Nerval, to be part of the wholeness of nature is desirable, but also possibly dangerous, since one cannot be sure that the whole is good ('Le Christ aux Oliviers', 'Vers Dorés'). The touch of fire is exciting and life-giving, but one may also be burned, for fire is dangerous ('Myrtho', 'Horus'). So love itself is both delight and torment, and such joys as it brings are not the simple ones of 'le bonheur' which he momentarily yearns for in *Sylvie*. The lady with the 'rose trémière' reappears in one of the visions of *Aurélia* (I, 374):

> La dame que je suivais, développant sa taille élancée dans un mouve-ment qui faisait miroiter les plis de sa robe en taffetas changeant, entoura gracieusement de son bras nu une longue tige de rose trémière, puis elle se mit à grandir sous un clair rayon de lumière, de telle sorte que peu à peu le jardin prenait sa forme, et les parterres et les arbres devenaient les rosaces et les festons de ses vêtements; tandis que sa figure et ses bras imprimaient leurs contours aux nuages pourprés du ciel. Je la perdais de vue à mesure qu'elle se transfigurait, car elle semblait s'évanouir dans sa propre grandeur. «Oh! ne fuis pas! m'écriai-je . . . car la nature meurt avec toi!»

There seems to be no doubt that 'celle que j'aimais seul' is indeed a goddess, in whom is resumed the whole of nature; and the phrase 'car elle semblait s'évanouir dans sa propre grandeur' recalls the description of the mother-goddess in *Isis* (I, 301), as she takes her leave of Lucius: 'l'invincible déesse disparaît et se recueille dans sa propre immensité'.[114] However, in *Aurélia* (I, 385) the phrase is applied again, with a slightly different tonality, to the god of Lucretius, 'impuissant et perdu dans son immensité'. The goddess is *invincible*; the god is *impuissant*. One is remin-ded of 'Horus', in which the green-eyed mother-goddess derides the dying Kneph, 'ce vieux pervers'. And just as 'Horus' ends with the flight of the goddess ('La déesse avait fui . . .'), so does the vision of *Aurélia* ('Oh! ne fuis pas!'). The beloved with the 'rose trémière' cannot offer a perfect consolation, but only a blend of *délice* and *tourment*.

Yet even this is not the worst of the poet's problems. Eternal love, despite its sorrows, offers at least a certainty. But what if death should prove to be not a continuation but an end? The vision in *Aurélia* ends with a sense of loss and the presence of death and darkness: 'portant les yeux autour de moi, je vis que le jardin avait pris l'aspect d'un cime-tière. Des voix disaient: "L'Univers est dans la nuit!"' The problem is the one which Pascal analyses so well: those who believe in God's existence will see God everywhere; but one cannot demonstrate the existence of God in the works of nature to those who do not already firmly believe in it, 'ces personnes destituées de foi et de grâce, qui, recherchant de toute leur lumière tout ce qu'ils voient dans la nature qui

les peut mener à cette connaissance, ne trouvent qu'obscurité et ténè-
bres'.[115] Such darkness shrouds the universe in this passage of *Aurélia*,
despite the presence of the goddess; it is the darkness of the 'puits sombre'
of 'Le Christ aux Oliviers', and indeed the poet's cry 'la nature meurt
avec toi' recalls the despair of Christ: 'Hélas! et si je meurs, c'est que
tout va mourir!' The uncertainty about the existence of God and the
immortality of the soul which one finds in 'Le Christ aux Oliviers' is
present also in 'Artémis'; and with it comes the temptation to fling life
away. If death is indeed an end, one cannot contemplate it with un-
mixed confidence; and yet, if one is unhappy, one would be tempted to
hasten it, too; for what is the point of suffering in life if one is not to find
in death even that balance of *délice* and *tourment* which is all that one can
hope for from love?

The first tercet moves on to consider this very possibility:

> Sainte napolitaine aux mains pleines de feux,
> Rose au cœur violet, fleur de sainte Gudule:
> As-tu trouvé ta croix dans le désert des cieux?

The first two lines of this tercet place side by side, without explanation,
a southern and a northern saint, one from Naples and the other from
Brussels. A variant on the Lombard manuscript reads 'sœur de sainte
Gudule', which makes the link between them explicit. Since Gudule had
a real sister (Sainte Reinelde), Nerval may have decided to rely on the
structure of the tercet: *as-tu trouvé* is in the singular, and makes it clear
that the two are one. He may also have wished to improve the sound and
reinforce the unity of the lines, for *fleur* not only avoids the excessive
sibilance of 'sœur de sainte', but also echoes *cœur* without offering too
close a similarity to the eye, and reminds one of *feux*. The lines sing like a
litany, a recital of the attributes of a divine figure. If we attempt to
explain their precise reference by separating the linked names, we
ignore the obvious intention to emphasise precisely the fact that they are
linked, to stress the identity of the two saints: this assertion that two are
one echoes the first quatrain.

The reference to Naples brings us back to the landscape of 'Delfica'
and 'Myrtho', and of *Octavie*. It has been suggested that the 'mains
pleines de feux' belong to the embroideress in *Octavie*, in whose room the
poet saw the cloths she worked on, 'un beau désordre d'étoffes brillantes'.
But there is nothing saint-like about this strange girl who appeared
'royalement parée' with 'des ornements de fausses pierres, colliers,
bracelets, couronne' (I, 288–9). One might identify the 'sainte napoli-
taine' with the 'enchanteresse' of 'Myrtho', a symbolic figure com-
pounded of the embroideress and Octavie, who had offered the poet the
fires of the volcano. It would then be the girl's likeness to the 'magi-
ciennes de Thessalie', and Octavie's portrayal of the goddess Isis, which

provide a link with the 'sainte de l'abîme,' of the final line: this is the goddess in her incarnation as 'la reine des mânes'; Nerval notes her other names, Diana Dictynna, whom the Greeks called 'the Cretan Artemis', and Hecate, that is, Artemis the goddess of the underworld and of magic (*Isis*; I, 301).

The image of the 'mains pleines de feux' also recalls certain Baroque statues of saints, in which the figure holds a monstrance surrounded by metal rays symbolising light, or Baroque paintings in which light streams from a holy figure; and it is like Yousouf's description, in *Voyage en Orient* (II, 366), of the woman he saw in his dreams: 'ses mains transparentes s'étendaient vers moi s'effilant en rayons de lumière'. The usual attribute of Sainte Gudule was a lantern, so that she also appears as a 'Sainte . . . aux mains pleines de feux'.[116] On the other hand, the figure of Sainte Rosalie which the poet saw in Naples was crowned with *roses violettes* (*Octavie*; I, 288), and the *rose au cœur violet* is here described as 'fleur de Sainte Gudule'. The attributes of the two saints are seen as interchangeable, reinforcing their unity. Describing the church of Sainte Gudule in Brussels,[117] Nerval remarks indeed that its magnificent Renaissance windows 'vous font rêver en plein Brabant l'horizon bleu de l'Italie, traversé de figures divines' (*Lorely*; II, 814).

Having evoked the two-fold saint, the poet has a question to ask her: 'As-tu trouvé ta croix dans le désert des cieux?' The words 'ta croix' seem to imply 'the one you expected to find'; but the question, like all the many questions in *Les Chimères*, is ambiguous, for it may also be asking 'did you find your cross there—or somewhere else?' In either case, though the question remains unanswered, the poet has clearly contemplated the possibility that the answer may be No. It is essentially the same question as the one with which Christ doubted the existence of God in 'Le Christ aux Oliviers': 'As-tu pouvoir de vivre et de vaincre la mort?'; and indeed, 'le désert des cieux' recalls the image of 'le sol désert' in the description of the purposeless universe in that poem. In *Aurélia* (I, 394) Nerval comments: 'Le désespoir et le suicide sont le résultat de certaines situations fatales pour qui n'a pas foi dans l'immortalité, dans ses peines et dans ses joies'. That is, even if one does believe in eternal life, the prospect is not one of paradisal bliss; it offers the poet both *peines* and *joies*: in the terms of this sonnet, both *délice* and *tourment*. But if one cannot believe in eternal life, with its promise of a love not subject to the vagaries of human time, the soul is left in despair, and the only rational solution is suicide.

For the moment, the poet reacts to doubt with the defiance of 'Antéros'. Since there is no certainty of eternal love, he refuses to count on it or to hope for it. The white roses which signal Heaven's pardon to Faust, in the Second Part of Goethe's play, are here scornfully rejected, and their Heaven too:

> Roses blanches, tombez! vous insultez nos dieux:
> Tombez fantômes blancs de votre ciel qui brûle:
> —La sainte de l'abîme est plus sainte à mes yeux!

The poet proclaims his allegiance to other gods; and he is not alone, since he speaks of '*nos* dieux'. We cannot know who his companion is (there may, of course, be more than one). It may be the other of 'Horus', who watched Isis depart ('la mer *nous* renvoyait son image adorée'), or the other addressed in 'Antéros', who seems to be ourselves ('Tu demandes . . .'). It may be the other to whom the imperative *Aimez* is addressed, who again may be the reader, or the poet himself; or it may be the *sainte*, or the *reine* whose lover he is, 'celle que j'aimai seul'. There is nothing problematical in all this, for all women are one woman, all men one man, and all beings linked in one vast soul. What matters here is the refusal to accept that this unity is governed by the heaven of the white roses. The white roses are white ghosts, dead, colourless things, cold like the dying Kneph, and like him rejected. They lack the passion of Isis and of Antéros, and the supreme temerity that drove Icarus and Phaeton towards the sun, and Christ to the *voûte éternelle*. The poet rejects them in favour of the *sainte de l'abîme*, who is as far removed as possible from the heaven of the white roses, like Baal and Dagon in their hell, and Cain in the mountain of Kaf. The spirit of revolt which prefers the *abîme* is found in a 'Faust'-like fragment by Nerval, *Nicolas Flamel*, first published in 1831 (see O.C. III, 346), where Satan speaks of 'deux principes contraires, mais égaux en gloire et en grandeur', and cries 'Un mont est quelque chose de beau, n'est-ce pas? un abîme l'est-il moins?'

The Eluard manuscript of this sonnet has a note in Nerval's hand beside the final verse: 'Rosalie'. She is the saint of the *roses violettes* which contrast so strongly with the *roses blanches*. But the 'sainte de l'abîme' is also Artémis herself, who as Hecate was goddess of the Underworld, of Death and of Night; while as Diana the huntress (whose figure appeared on the Renaissance clock in *Sylvie*) she was goddess of the moon and of chastity.[118] In a discussion of Euripides' play *Hippolytus*,[119] Nerval recounts the death of the hero, who was punished by Venus, goddess of earthly love, for his obstinate devotion to Diana; invoking death with cries of pain, Hippolytus is calmed and soothed by the approach of 'la divine Diane'. Nerval calls her 'Diane la vierge sainte', and comments on Hippolytus' death: 'c'est le martyr mourant consolé par la sainte en qui il a foi'. The ancient goddess and the Christian saint and virgin are one. Moreover, that the poet should turn to Diana is less paradoxical than it might seem, for she is by no means a cold and lifeless deity, for all her chastity. Nerval includes her among the avatars of Isis, the goddess-mother, and she is equivalent to the goddess Venus also (that is, to the mystical Venus),[120] as Isis told Lucius (*Isis*; I, 301):

> moi, la mère de la nature, la maîtresse des éléments, la source première des siècles, la plus grande des divinités, la reine des mânes . . . l'on me nomme en Phrygie, Cybèle; à Athènes, Minerve; en Chypre, Vénus Paphienne; en Crète, Diane Dictynne; en Sicile, Proserpine Stygienne; à Eleusis, l'antique Cérès . . .

Love and chastity go hand in hand; indeed, chastity is only fidelity to the highest kind of love (and here Artémis can be seen to include the figure of Arthémise, the faithful widow of Mausolus).[121] Such is the fidelity which Isis requires, and immortality depends on this constant love (I, 301):

> tu dois me consacrer le reste de ta vie, et, dès que tu auras franchi le sombre bord, tu ne cesseras encore de m'adorer, soit dans les ténèbres de l'Achéron ou dans les Champs-Elysées; et si, par l'observation de mon culte et par une inviolable chasteté, tu mérites bien de moi, tu sauras que je puis seule prolonger ta vie spirituelle au delà des bornes marquées.

Purity and love, Diana and Venus, were inseparable for Nerval. Not only did he see chastity as the highest expression of love, but conversely, through perfect love one could reach a perfect purity. Nerval touches several times on the favourite Romantic theme of the rehabilitation of the prostitute through love; the figure of Mary Magdalene is the archetypal symbol of this notion, and Nerval refers to her more than once in his note-books. The courtesan Vasantasena was similarly redeemed by love; she is the heroine of *Le Chariot d'Enfant*, an Indian drama adapted by Nerval in collaboration with Méry, and performed in 1850. A note among the fragments known as *Voyage d'Italie—Panorama* (I. 425) seems to stem from a personal concern:

> Si le Pape lui pardonnait . . .
>
> Une larme de Marie qui tombe sur son front.
>
> Je voudrais la laver dans une piscine grande comme
>
> l'Océan—des idées d'expiation—Le Monde ne pardonne pas.

The *Lettres à Jenny Colon* also suggest that a truly dedicated love can redeem and cancel out even those attachments which ordinary lovers might regard as infidelities: 'pour ce qui est de la jalousie, c'est un côté bien mort chez moi'; 'Que m'importe que vous ayez été à d'autres, que vous soyez à d'autres peut-être!'. The love he imagined bore no resemblance to 'la galanterie ordinaire': 'Vous êtes la première femme que j'aime et je suis peut-être le premier homme qui vous aime à ce point. Si ce n'est pas là une sorte d'hymen que le ciel bénisse, le mot amour n'est qu'un vain mot!' (I, 755, 758). The idea is most clearly presented in *L'Imagier de Harlem*, with which 'Artémis' has so many links. Laurent Coster offers Alilah (here disguised as Anne de Beaujeu) redemption through his love for her, and almost succeeds in breaking the spell that binds her to the Devil; he speaks as if he were snatching her back from the dead:[122]

> Je sens, femme sans nom, que ma vie en t'aimant
> Passera dans ta vie, et que, dès ce moment,
> Du domaine infernal franchissant les limites,
> Ombre tu prends un corps! morte, tu ressuscites!

It becomes clear that 'la morte' of 'Artémis', 'celle que j'aimai seul', depends for her existence on the poet's love (as the goddess does in 'Horus'). At the same time, his constancy in love is his own justification, and his only hope of salvation and immortality: hence the imperative 'Aimez!'.

Yet the way to salvation is by no means easy, for love is not easy. Alilah is overjoyed at first to take her place among the 'tendresses humaines', but then is filled with fear: 'Ne m'aime pas; ce mot est rempli de frissons' (O.C. V, 138). The poet is evidently still as afraid of the dangers of love as he was when he wrote 'Vers Dorés' and 'Myrtho'; and he knows that fear is the greatest obstacle to his victory, as it was for Adoniram.

There can be little doubt that 'Artémis' contemplates with unblinking clarity a despair that the other sonnets of *Les Chimères* hold in a delicate balance. Its structure reflects this, for whereas the other sonnets generally offer in their final tercet a counterweight of some kind to the forces built up in the first eleven lines, 'Artémis' broods over the same dark vision from first to last. Yet even here there are glimpses of an answer. It lies in the ambiguity of *la rose*. The rose can console, like the *fleur* of 'El Desdichado', with its 'treille où le pampre à rose s'allie'. It is also the dark 'Rose au cœur violet', associated with the 'roses violettes' which crown the statue of Sainte Rosalie in *Octavie*. As François Constans has pointed out, Nerval found this symbol in the German writer Hoffmann;[123] the violet rose stands for love, guilt and punishment, followed by a hope of final redemption. That hope seems to be questioned in 'Artémis'. The only certain rose here is the *rose trémière*, which the vision of Aurélia held as she beckoned the poet to follow her, and whose name is yet so oddly suggestive of trembling hesitation and fear. The equilibrium which is glimpsed in 'Artémis' is the balance of eternal ambiguity, in which first is last, many are one, delight is torment, and hell is holy. Yet we are not left with a sense of ultimate despair, but rather with the feeling that the poet has contemplated death, even death at his own hand, and seen it as part of a pattern. His final word seems to be contained in the second quatrain: *Aimez*. Echoed four times within the sonnet by the words *amant*, *aima*, *aimai*, *aime*, the imperative urges the necessity of love. Though it does not bring happiness in everyday terms, it is the force that, according to 'Vers Dorés', links all things in *un mystère d'amour*. But love, as Nerval conceives it, is not a Heaven-sent gift; it demands a positive effort: the blood-red rose which symbolises redemption through love and suffering seems to the poet more holy than the cold white roses of a proffered grace. This rebel will accept his God gladly if God will accept his right to find his own way to salvation and certainty; and that way lies not through the passive acceptance of authority but through doubt and anguish to perfect love.

The association of perfect love with chastity and death (and Diana is goddess of both) has led many critics (following notably the example of L.-H. Sebillotte)[124] to see 'Artémis' as a poem of impotence, a poem that prefers an idealised love because it is written by a man who was incapable of a 'normal' human love. There is undoubtedly an element of truth in such analyses of Nerval's personality, but not so entire a truth that we can be content to substitute it for the poem's own truth. This sonnet was written by a poet who was trying to create an order, not by a man who was trying to record a disorder. The failure that 'Artémis' records is more profound and more far-reaching than sexual impotence. For there can be no doubt that this sonnet records a failure. It has the tone of rebellion which one finds in 'Antéros', but not the confidence.

Nerval's friend Arsène Houssaye, editor of *L'Artiste* (in which many of Nerval's poems were first published), wrote a short piece in that journal (15 January 1853) which oddly echoes 'Artémis'. Houssaye quotes a writer named Chevreau as having said 'Aime toujours l'amour qui t'aime', and he comments with his habitual cynicism: 'Aimer qui ne vous aime pas, c'est l'amour; aimer qui vous aime, ce serait le paradis'. Clearly Houssaye doubts the likelihood of such a paradise. In 'Artémis', Nerval repeats Chevreau's injunction: 'Aimez qui vous aima . . .'; but the love he envisages belongs, precisely, to 'le paradis', where the poet and 'la morte' will be united, each one the only lover of the other. The failure of 'Artémis' lies in the fact that this love is essentially an exclusive love, like that described in 'Horus' and in 'Antéros', where mother-goddess and child are united, defying the dangerous power of God the Father. In 'Artémis' also, God seems to be rejected. But there is no joy in that rejection, only a desperate hope. With his constant need for unity and reconciliation, Nerval must have been aware that true reconciliation would embrace not only 'qui vous aime', but also 'qui ne vous aime pas'. Cain must forgive Adonai, as Prometheus forgave Jupiter, and was thus reconciled, and set free from the worst of all chains: the inability to love.[125] Perfect love implies perfect trust and perfect forgiveness; and it is absent from 'Artémis'. It will not be achieved until Nerval comes to write *Memorabilia*, in which even the terrifying gods of fire are pardoned and blessed with love.

This sonnet is in fact a poetic condensation of the moral and emotional questions which are raised in *Aurélia*. Its extreme concentration makes it the most difficult of the sonnets; unlike its companions, it does not proceed from a specific landscape or experience, nor does it obviously dramatise a myth. Its subject is experience itself, as we know it in time and as we conceive it might be in eternity. For this vast theme, the sonnet form seems paradoxically to be the most eminently suitable vehicle. Its little space, in which images, sounds and rhythms echo and resound, focuses time and the universe as a burning-glass focuses the rays of the sun on a single point, and with the same intensity.

EL DESDICHADO

The sonnet (p. 43) which Nerval placed at the head of *Les Chimères* was first published in *Le Mousquetaire*, 10 December 1853. This journal was directed by his friend Alexandre Dumas. According to the note which Dumas printed by way of introduction to the poem, Nerval had called at the journal's offices, and finding that Dumas was out, had left 'El Desdichado' as a visiting card ('Je suis . . .'). Dumas seems to suggest that Nerval had actually composed the sonnet on the spot, as a kind of *jeu d'esprit*. He refers to the fact that by the time the sonnet appeared in print, Nerval was confined in the clinic of Dr Emile Blanche; his remarks constitute virtually an epitaph for the poet's sanity. Nerval might equally have been writing out from memory a poem composed long before, but it is clear that Dumas was concerned to explain away the sonnet's apparent obscurity by hinting that its author was not mentally stable at the time, or alternatively that the poem was not intended to be taken seriously. Not unnaturally, Nerval objected strongly to both insinuations, as he had objected in 1841 when Jules Janin made a similar mistake. In the preface to *Les Filles du Feu* Nerval refers ironically to his two 'obituaries' (I, 149), and it seems likely that both *Les Filles du Feu* and *Les Chimères*, like the various other collected writings published by the poet at this time, were intended to convince the public that Nerval was still in control of his mind and of his pen. But besides his general effort to consolidate the work of a lifetime, he seems especially concerned that 'El Desdichado' should not appear out of its true context. It is clear that Nerval did not think that this sonnet could stand alone: 'puisque vous avez eu l'imprudence de citer un des sonnets . . . il faut que vous les entendiez tous' (I, 158).

It is likely that 'El Desdichado' was the last of the sonnets to be written, though we cannot establish with certainty its relation to 'Artémis', since the only known unpublished versions of 'El Desdichado' (the Lombard and Eluard manuscripts) are accompanied in each case by versions of

'Artémis'. The sonnet as published by Dumas differs in one or two details from the version which appeared very shortly afterwards in *Les Filles du Feu* (January 1854); some, but not all, of these variants appear on the Lombard manuscript. The circumstances of its first publication, as related by Dumas, were such that Nerval would have been unable to correct the proofs of his poem; the variants in *Le Mousquetaire* may thus be errors (or alterations) made by Dumas—it is impossible to tell.

In 1952, 'Artémis' was described as the sonnet which had attracted the most attention among the poems of *Les Chimères*.[126] That distinction now seems to have passed to 'El Desdichado'. This sonnet does not present the obvious syntactical difficulties which we find in 'Artémis': the problem is not to decide what is being said, but to decide where the emphasis lies. The statements made in 'El Desdichado' are plain (and in this it seems to resemble 'Vers Dorés' or 'Le Christ aux Oliviers' rather than 'Artémis'); but the relations between those statements are not at all plain, so that the mood of the poem is not easily defined. Nerval placed it first in the sequence, so that it acts as a kind of preface to *Les Chimères*; and it does in fact sum up the themes which appear in the other sonnets. However, as we shall see, it also marks a definite step forward from the position of its companions, and on that ground alone it seems reasonable to suggest that it may be the last of the sonnets. Certainly it seems to date from late in the poet's life: looking backwards over the ground the poet has covered, it appears to be closing the account.

The structure of 'El Desdichado' is if possible even more consciously controlled than that of the sonnets it introduces. Its pattern most resembles that of 'Artémis': each quatrain and each tercet appears to stand alone, examining the poet's thought from a different angle: yet there is movement from one to the next, whose direction we finally perceive only when the whole has been placed before us. If these two sonnets have elicited the most comment, it is because in each of them the logical connections between the parts are not made obvious by grammatical links. No *aussi*, no *mais*, no *depuis*, no *cependant*, no *c'est que*, no obvious thread of narrative, no dialogue, nothing is offered which might help us—or tempt us—to construct a linear sequence of any kind. The tenses of the verbs wander from present to past and back again; and present includes past and suggests an eternal future, being linked in both these sonnets with the adverb *encor*: 'Celle que j'aimai seul *m'aime encor* tendrement'; 'Mon front *est rouge encor* du baiser de la reine'. We are thus forced to accept the sonnet as an object whose parts have meaning only in relation to the whole. This is as true of 'El Desdichado' as it is of 'Artémis', despite the fact that it appears at first to be easier to grasp. In 'Artémis', some of the elements are so veiled as to be easily missed: the sonnet is moving towards darkness. By contrast, 'El Desdichado' begins in darkness and moves towards the light. Both sonnets, however, have the same self-contained structure, turned in upon itself at every point, each word illuminated by all the others. Like 'Artémis', 'El Desdichado' is not a sequence, but a circle. Where words or ideas are arranged in a linear progression, the mind assumes that the progression could be extended beyond its present limits. The words in 'El Desdichado', as in 'Artémis', react with each other and explore a shifting pattern of meaning; but the movement is circumscribed by the formal pattern of the sonnet, which contains the references of the words within a precisely defined and coherent universe.

The sonnet's title has been the subject of much comment, though as a title it is no more mysterious than 'Delfica' or 'Myrtho', which likewise do not refer to known historical or mythological figures. The commonly accepted source is Sir Walter Scott's novel *Ivanhoe*, in which a knight whose lands are seized by King John chooses 'El Desdichado' as his device: it means 'disinherited' according to Scott, though some authorities claim that it actually means only 'unhappy'. Another possible, and more likely source, is Lesage's novel *Le Diable boiteux*, which Nerval refers to as the 'fameux Diable boiteux que nous connaissons tous'.[127] A. Kies points out that in this novel a noble gentleman, don Blaz Desdichado, losing his right to his wife's fortune when she dies, loses his reason also, and is thus disinherited, *veuf*, and *inconsolé*.[128] Neither of these sources tells us any more about the sonnet than the title itself, and it is reasonable to suppose that Nerval did not intend his sonnet to direct our attention to any source outside itself, but merely chose the title because it expressed what he wanted to express: that feeling of being *déshérité* which we have already met in 'Delfica' and in 'Antéros'. The sonnet contains within itself all we need to understand it; it would be equally valid without its title, and indeed one manuscript version bears the alternative title 'Le Destin'. One can say, however, that the name of this sonnet, unlike those of its companions, strikes a mediaeval or courtly rather than a classical note, introducing a new point of time intermediate between the present and antiquity.

The first quatrain echoes both the mediaeval and the melancholy aspects of the title:

Je suis le ténébreux,—le veuf,—l'inconsolé . . .

The curiously halting movement of the line isolates each of the epithets in a brooding silence; and the following line rocks back and forth in the same dark sorrow:

Le prince d'Aquitaine à la tour abolie . . .

Only now are we given a hint of the cause of this grief:

Ma seule *étoile* est morte,—et mon luth constellé
Porte le *Soleil noir* de la *Mélancolie*.

The total impression of darkness and tragic loss is so strong that one does not at this point question the origin of the symbols. That they are symbols is made clear by the poet's use of the definite article to give them a representative quality, and of capital letters and italic print to isolate and enlarge them. He thus gives to his dark bereavement an allegorical force. This is not just a melancholy man, but '*le* veuf, *l*'inconsolé', the essence of loss and the epitome of grief.

The epithets immediately recall Brisacier's description of himself in the preface to *Les Filles du Feu* (I, 152): 'moi . . . le prince ignoré, l'amant mystérieux, le déshérité, le banni de liesse, le beau ténébreux . . .'; and Brisacier himself refers to Scarron's *Roman comique*, whose hero and heroine were named Le Destin (which is the alternative title of this sonnet) and L'Etoile (I, 151). In Scarron's novel, Le Destin suffers from the cold incomprehension of his father, and comforts himself with dreams of being in fact the son of an unknown aristocrat, perhaps even of royal blood (hence 'le prince ignoré'). We have seen that this fantasy is one which Nerval himself at times entertained: it lies behind 'Horus'. There is no explicit reference to Nerval's father in 'El Desdichado', but he seems nonetheless to be in the poet's mind. While 'Artémis' clearly fails to include 'celui qui ne vous aime pas' in the general reconciliation the poet was striving for, 'El Desdichado' seems to be trying to find a place for him. That may be why this sonnet has shifted in time, evoking the image of a troubadour, and of the kingdom of Aquitaine; for Nerval always associated his father with the south, and especially with Périgord and the chivalric traditions of that region. Biron, who is mentioned in the ninth line, is another image of Dr Labrunie: one member of the Biron family (to whom Nerval refers in *Chansons et Légendes du Valois*, I, 280) was a gallant soldier known to the people of France, who loved him, as Le Boiteux: he was lame, like Nerval's father (who had also been a soldier), and like the god Kneph in 'Horus'. In a letter to his father which he sent from Germany in May 1854 (I, 1110), Nerval recalls Dr Labrunie's military career and compares it to his own less glorious struggles; but he repeatedly stresses his likeness to his father at this time. In June he is amused to find that, like his father, he offends people by not recognising them in the street, being like Dr Labrunie shortsighted: 'tel père, tel fils' (I, 1119). Later the same month he confesses 'Plus j'avance en âge, plus je sens de toi en moi' (I, 1127). At this late stage in his life, he is evidently making a tremendous effort to remind himself that he is the child of his father as well as of his mother. The reference to Le Destin is thus not merely a reference to a romantic adventurer, but touches on a problem which Nerval is beginning to face consciously for the first time: the necessity of including 'celui qui ne vous aime pas' in his love. The first step is to identify himself with his father, and this sonnet begins in fact with such an identification: Nerval's father was a widower, and it can be no accident that Nerval here uses the word *veuf* to describe himself.

He is widowed because he has lost 'ma seule *étoile*'. It would limit the significance of this first quatrain to interpret the 'star' as the symbol of any particular woman. The final chapter of *Sylvie* speaks of the fading of 'les chimères qui charment et égarent au matin de la vie': 'Ermenonville!... tu as perdu ta seule étoile, qui chatoyait pour moi d'un double éclat. Tour à tour bleue et rose comme l'astre trompeur d'Aldébaran, c'était Adrienne ou Sylvie,—c'était les deux moitiés d'un seul amour' (I, 271–2). The 'seule étoile' is love itself, which is a 'chimère', an 'astre trompeur', a splendid, ambiguous image which the poet can now no longer see; and though he knows it to be an illusion, its loss profoundly disturbs him. It should be noted that this quatrain records not only a loss of love, but also a loss of identity, or at least a change of identity in so far as identity is established by heraldic devices: the poet is a prince whose tower, symbol of his heritage, has been destroyed; he is a troubadour whose lute bears an emblem now sadly changed from bright star to dark sun; what he is now ('Je suis . . .') is not what he was.

Yet dark as the poet's grief may be in the first quatrain, it is not without some indication of a possible relief. Despite the *tour abolie* and the *étoile . . . morte*, two verbs in the present tense affirm the poet's continuing existence and activity. The first two words of the sonnet are as firmly underlined as the epithets which describe the poet: '*Je suis* le ténébreux'. He still lives, and is still a poet: 'mon luth constellé *Porte* le *Soleil noir*'; the lute, the instrument of the poet's art, though darkened, is still in his hand. Perhaps in consequence of the evocation of the lute, the final line of the first quatrain has a smooth, softening movement, and the inherent sweetness of the word *Mélancolie* produces a muted sorrow entirely different from the solid darkness of the first line. We are thus prepared for the sudden light with which the second quatrain overflows.

The movement of the lines in the second quatrain is lighter, with a more rapid flow of images towards the end. The feeling becomes less profound. While *consolé* echoes the grief of the first quatrain, offering only a glimpse of light in the total darkness of 'la nuit du tombeau', light comes flooding in with the mention of 'le Pausilippe et la mer d'Italie'. In this context, 'mon cœur *désolé*' has none of the force of *l'inconsolé* in the opening lines of the sonnet. (It should be noted again how the definite article contributes to this effect: it gives to the poet's sorrow a representative, generalised quality, so that he seems to be not grieved, but grief itself—the word *désolé* is very slight in comparison.) In this second quatrain the sadness seems transient, almost sweet, blending easily with the sunlit landscape. One recalls the poet's mood on Posilipo, as he describes it in *Octavie* (I, 289–90):

> Arrivé tout en haut, je me promenais en regardant la mer déjà bleue, la ville où l'on n'entendait encore que les bruits du matin, et les îles de la baie, où le soleil commençait à dorer le haut des villas. Je n'étais pas attristé le moins du monde; je marchais à grands pas, je courais, je descendais les pentes, je me roulais dans l'herbe humide; mais dans mon cœur il y avait l'idée de la mort.

The sonnet has shown us so far two partly contradictory images: the poet in darkness and the poet in sunlight. However, it is essential to note that each quatrain contains the germ of the other. The first implies that the poet has *become* 'le ténébreux'; if he is 'veuf', he must once have been in possession of his joy. The second quatrain recognises the existence of sadness at the heart of joy, while recalling that the poet has once before emerged from darkness into light, and may therefore hope to do so again:

> Dans la nuit du tombeau, toi qui m'as consolé,
> Rends-moi le Pausilippe . . .

The syntax is marvellously ambiguous, embracing past, present and future in a timeless unity. The lines mean both 'Toi qui m'as consolé quand j'étais autrefois dans la nuit du tombeau, rends-moi maintenant le Pausilippe', and also 'Maintenant que je suis dans la nuit du tombeau, toi qui m'as consolé autrefois (ou cette fois-ci), rends-moi le Pausilippe'. The total effect is to make us feel that something which has happened before may perhaps happen again: it is possible at least, even if it seems at the moment unlikely. The movement thus appears to be, as in 'Delfica', a continuous alternation, in this case an alternating movement from darkness into light, and back again. Nerval recognised that the face of the world altered with his moods; and he used the image of the 'soleil noir' to symbolise this tendency. Describing the fascination of Egypt, he remarks: 'tout cela me surprend, me ravit . . . ou m'attriste, selon les jours; car je ne veux pas dire qu'un éternel été fasse une vie toujours joyeuse. Le soleil noir de la mélancolie, qui verse des rayons obscurs sur le front de l'ange rêveur d'Albert Dürer, se lève aussi parfois aux plaines lumineuses du Nil, comme sur les bords du Rhin . . .'[129] This profound change in the poet's vision of the world can be described without exaggeration as a change of identity, such as the first quatrain of 'El Desdichado' describes: from being 'starry' with the emblem of love and consolation, his lute and his song are suddenly brought under the sign of the *soleil noir*.

At this point one might ask to whom the word *toi* refers. The landscape evoked in this second quatrain is so strongly reminiscent of 'Myrtho' and 'Delfica' that one is inclined to identify *toi* with the 'divine enchanteresse' or with 'la fille blonde qui mange des citrons'[130] (who on one level at least are one and the same). It is interesting to note, in passing, that no mention whatever is made of light, sun or sky in this quatrain, yet the visual impression of brilliantly sunlit water is very strong, partly because of the images suggested by *la mer d'Italie*, partly because of the association with the 'Pausilippe altier, de mille feux brillant' of 'Myrtho'. The sudden movement away from darkness is underlined by the presence of *la fleur* and *la rose*. This precisely detailed context seems to set the scene of a drama; one cannot help feeling that *toi* is not an abstraction but a human being, and probably a woman. There is however nothing else in the sonnet which supports this identi-fication: if *toi* means a particular girl, this is the first and last mention of her. Furthermore, the 'treille où le pampre à la rose s'allie' may not refer only to the setting of an encounter in Italy; in *Sylvie* Nerval recalls the cottage in the Valois where Sylvie lived: 'Je revois sa fenêtre où le pampre s'enlace au rosier . . .' (I, 247).[131] It is much more likely that, like *ma seule étoile*, the word *toi* refers to love itself, symbolised here by the 'terre du feu', the Neapolitan landscape which serves to define it in 'Myrtho', and by the Valois which was the home of Angélique and Sylvie, 'filles du feu'.

There is another possible, and related, interpretation to be found in the sonnet: *toi* could refer to 'mon luth constellé'. This does not exclude the idea of love, and still links the poem with 'Myrtho', for the *ivresse* which Myrtho brings to the poet is the ecstasy of poetry as well as of love: 'Car *la Muse* m'a fait l'un des fils de la Grèce'. Moreover, while actual experience, or a particular woman, is unlikely to bring back Posilipo, the poet can re-create its presence, and the presence of love, in his poem. And indeed he does so: by the time we reach the end of the second quatrain, Posilipo is palpably there.

The first tercet now takes the assertion with which the poem began, and inverts it: 'Suis-je . . . ?' The four symbolic figures named in this line produce a sense of mystery; perhaps also, since it is framed as a question, a sense that the poet is confused. We become ourselves un-certain. It is not in the least clear what is the precise nature of the alternatives which the poet is considering. That they are alternatives seems plain; and it is thus most probable that their significance for the poet lies only in the qualities which make them alternative. In that case, no interpretation of any one of these symbols can be accepted if it does not fit into a pattern which will also include the others. The balance of the groups of syllables makes it difficult to read this line without pausing after *Amour* and after *Lusignan*. This creates two similar sets of possibilities (that is, 'Amour ou Phébus' is the same as 'Lusignan ou Biron'), suggesting at once that *Amour* and *Lusignan* have something in common, and that the alternative to that quality is the quality inherent in *Phébus* and *Biron*. At the same time, the fact that one pair of names derives from classical mythology and one from the legends of France, places the problem in the context of time. We are again reminded that, as in 'Delfica', the alternating movement implied in the quatrains can be repeated indefinitely.

Many different interpretations of the ninth line of this sonnet have been proposed, most of which depend on research into the various connotations of the four proper names it contains. Amour is the god Eros, brother of Antéros, the lover in darkness betrayed by Psyche. Phébus is Apollo, the god of light, of divination and of poetry. Lusignan was a mediaeval lord who married the fairy Mélusine and lost her because he did not trust her (as Psyche lost Eros because she did not trust him). Biron is the gay figure of legend and song to whom Nerval refers in the *Chansons et Légendes du Valois* (I, 280). He is also the poet Byron: the version of this sonnet published in *Le Mousquetaire* has *Byron*, while an early poem of Nerval's ('A Napoléon') is subtitled *Traduit de Lord Biron*;[132] so that it would appear that Biron is a Don Juan-like figure, a gay and successful lover, as opposed to Amour and Lusignan—that was part of the image of Byron as the French Romantics saw him, and that is how Nerval speaks of him in *Voyage en Orient*.[133] All this information does not seem however to make the sonnet much clearer, since it is the relations between these figures which really matter. By pursuing their individual meanings too far we disperse them: whereas the sonnet has linked them closely together. It is possible in fact to place this line within the context of the sonnet as a whole, without defining the precise nature of the four symbolic figures. The quatrains have already offered us an alternative which might be expressed as 'isolation or consolation', or possibly as 'melancholy or joy', or even more simply as 'darkness or light'. It is not unreasonable to suppose that the first tercet continues to consider this alternative. This would give us a structure in which the first eleven lines are balanced against the last three, as in 'Delfica', 'Myrtho', 'Horus', 'Antéros' and 'Artémis'. The first quatrain asserts 'I am darkness'; the second remembers 'but I have been light'; the first tercet goes on quite logically to ask 'then which of these two things am I?'

The remaining lines of the first tercet appear to be continuing to reflect on alternative possibilities; but in fact they subtly alter the mood of the poem. The uncertainty caused by the unexpected question 'Suis-je . . .?' is rapidly dissipated here by two positive statements. These statements, which seem intended to help to define what the poet is, are offered as equally valid. No connection is made between them; they simply stand side by side:

Mon front est rouge encor du baiser de la reine;
J'ai rêvé dans la grotte où nage la syrène . . .

The alternative seems less and less to imply a contradiction. The parallel construction of these lines begins to suggest not 'I am this or that', but 'I am this *and* that'. As in 'Artémis', the word *ou* expresses not a radical difference, but another aspect of the same unchanging object. Again, the precise connotations of the images matter less than the relationships between them which the poem creates. The 'baiser de la reine' has a mediaeval colouring which links it with the 'prince d'Aquitaine' of the first quatrain; while 'la grotte où nage la syrène' belongs to classical mythology and the world of 'Delfica' and 'Myrtho'. This tercet effects a fusion between the diverse elements of the quatrains, which were, it will be remembered, already linked in that there was some overlapping of the two areas of experience they describe. As the poem progresses, the co-existence of these areas of experience seems to be increasingly realised: 'Mon front est rouge *encor*' implies 'this experience is still with me'; and in 'J'ai rêvé dans la grotte', the perfect tense relates the action very closely to the present time (as in 'J'ai revêtu pour lui la robe de Cybèle'), implying 'I am this dreamer'.

This tercet does, however, introduce a new consideration. Like 'Artémis', it is asking questions not only about the poet's identity, but also about his lover's. Here again there appears to be an alternative: there is an obvious contrast between *reine* and *syrène*. The image of 'la reine' suggests majesty and nobility; her kiss has left the poet for ever marked with the sign of a privileged moment, it has in some way consecrated him. The 'baiser de la reine' recalls the children's game in *Sylvie* (I, 245–6), in which the young Nerval exchanged a kiss with Adrienne. He thought of her as a kind of queen, since she was 'petite-fille de l'un des descendants d'une famille alliée aux anciens rois de France'; he crowns her with laurel, and she appears to him like 'la Béatrice de Dante qui sourit au poète errant sur la lisière des saintes demeures'. He feels himself to be utterly changed by the kiss: 'De ce moment, un trouble inconnu s'empara de moi'; the phrase 'de ce moment' seems to imply that he is troubled still: 'Mon front est rouge encor . . .' In contrast to this radiant image, the 'syrène' conjures up a vision of dark and dangerous waters, of 'la grotte fatale aux hôtes imprudents', of the beautiful Aspasie, 'naïade du Cocyte'. The version of this sonnet published in *Le Mousquetaire* has 'J'ai *dormi* dans la grotte où *verdit* la sirène', which recalls the reference, in a passage of *Voyage en Orient* (II, 87) dealing with the death of the ancient gods, to 'La verte naïade . . . dans sa grotte'. The siren represents the fascination of foreknown disaster, and the treachery of betrayal by what seems both beautiful and kind. Her image runs right through Nerval's work from first to last, often veiled or touched upon unwillingly. She stands for everything in woman that is both deadly and delightful; she casts a spell, but the spell can kill.

The two images are not, however, truly in opposition. Woman is essentially both *reine* and *syrène*. The Eluard manuscript has 'Reine Candace' against the tenth line; it is another name for Balkis, Queen of Sheba, the lover of Adoniram, and like him a child of fire. Nerval tells their story in *Voyage en Orient*. The radiant figure of the queen is by no means unambiguous. The artist Adoniram is granted the 'baiser de la reine', but he pays for it with his life; the story suggests, as 'Myrtho' does, that the touch of fire can be deadly.[134] Nerval compares Balkis (II, 518–21) to 'l'idéale et mystique figure de la déesse Isis', but remarks also 'cette expression fine, railleuse et hautaine avec enjouement des personnes de très grande lignée habituées à la domination'; she has 'les traits de la plus enivrante beauté', but also 'un profil . . . où rayonne un œil noir' (like that in Heine's poem 'Le Naufragé' which is linked with 'Myrtho');[135] she has a 'coquetterie prévoyante'; and the poet remembers her eyes 'que la malice animait plus que l'amour' (*Petits Châteaux de Bohême*; I, 71). In an article, 'Le Boulevard du Temple—Aujourd'hui', published in *L'Artiste* (1844), Nerval describes an acrobat who reminds him of both *reine* and *syrène*: 'cette jolie fille aux cheveux rouges . . . tout son corps se repliait en queue de dauphin, image classique de l'antique sirène! Oh! ses cheveux aux ondes pourprées, comme ceux de la reine de Saba!' (O.C. VIII, 70).

Woman, or love itself, has a double nature. All women are like the girl in *Octavie*, 'ce fantôme qui me séduisait et m'effrayait à la fois' (I, 289). But if woman can be these two contradictory things 'à la fois', it would be reasonable to suppose that the alternative images of the poet himself need not be mutually exclusive. The ninth line does not in fact state 'If I am this I cannot be that'. Indeed, being framed as a question, it states nothing: it merely examines the various possibilities in turn and tries to understand how they can be made to relate to each other.

The constant alternation described in the quatrains might be seen as creating a relation between the poet's selves which is a purely temporal one: the dark self alternates with the light, in the same way as the gods eternally replace each other in 'Delfica'. Such a relation would be both unstable and unpredictable, and the poet must try to create a genuine and timeless synthesis between his two selves, in the same way as 'Myrtho' attempts to unite the green myrtle and the pale hydrangea.

The final tercet achieves a synthesis of this kind between the two feminine figures evoked in the tenth and eleventh lines. It begins, however, with a statement about the poet himself:

> Et j'ai deux fois vainqueur traversé l'Achéron . . .

The *Et* makes it clear that there is no disjunction here: this is a statement about the poet's identity parallel to those in the tenth and eleventh lines. His victory has not been won *in spite of* the conflicting experiences he has recorded in this sonnet, but in some way *through* them; it is a continuation, even a confirmation, of them. In the closing lines of 'El Desdichado' there is a sense that all conflict is resolved, and an assurance unlike anything else in *Les Chimères*, summed up in the one word *vainqueur*:

> Et j'ai deux fois vainqueur traversé l'Achéron . . .

The claim is so unemphatically made that one might easily miss its implications. This is not merely (as in the 'Ils m'ont plongé trois fois dans les eaux du Cocyte' of 'Antéros') a test of strength which leaves the poet defiant, and anxious to assert the values of love and hope. It is a genuine victory, achieved in the course of a descent into 'la nuit du tombeau' and a painful return. The sonnet tells us, moreover, how this victory was achieved:

> Modulant tour à tour sur la lyre d'Orphée
> Les soupirs de la sainte et les cris de la fée.

There is an echo, in these two feminine figures, of those in the first tercet; one feels that the same kind of tension exists between *sainte* and *fée* as between *reine* and *syrène*.[136] But it is now clear that just as each of the two worlds of the quatrains contains the germ of the other, so the two feminine figures are not essentially opposed. In this final tercet all sense of conflict in the alternation has gone. 'Modulant *tour à tour* . . .': the poet's victory has come from his acceptance of the dual nature of woman, who is both *reine* and *syrène*, both *sainte* and *fée*; he has accepted, that is, that the *délice* and the *tourment* of love, whose complex interaction troubled him in 'Artémis', are two inseparable aspects of the same experience. This is the attitude he commended in Heine (O.C. I, 89):

> Ce qu'il y a de beau dans Henri Heine, c'est qu'il ne se fait pas illusion; il accepte la femme telle qu'elle est, il l'aime malgré ses défauts et surtout à cause de ses défauts; heureux ou malheureux, accepté ou refusé, il sait qu'il va souffrir et il ne recule pas . . .

The implication of a fear overcome recalls the 'vainqueur' of 'El Desdichado'.

The poet's victory is not however solely concerned with his recognition of the nature of woman. Having accepted the duality of his lover, the poet can go on to accept that he himself may be both Amour and Phébus, both Lusignan and Biron. It takes little imagination to see that the acceptance of this idea might be difficult, since it is contrary to all our notions of consistency and strength of character. Yet it offers the very solution that the poet has been seeking. The question 'Suis-je . . .' echoes obscurely the questions of 'Artémis':

> Car es-tu reine, ô toi! la première ou dernière?
>
> Es-tu roi, toi le seul ou le dernier amant?

In 'El Desdichado', however, the poet's first preoccupation is with his own identity; he has become aware that the root of his problem lies in the complexities of his nature.[137] In a late sonnet, 'Epitaphe' (I, 44), he acknowledges that his temperament is subject to alternating moods, and he expresses the duality, exactly as in 'El Desdichado', by means of contrasting images of gay and melancholy lovers:

> Il a vécu tantôt gai comme un sansonnet,
>
> Tour à tour amoureux insoucieux et tendre,
>
> Tantôt sombre et rêveur comme un triste Clitandre . . .

It is no accident that the phrase *tour à tour* occurs both here and in 'El Desdichado', as it does in his description of love in *Sylvie* (I, 272): 'seule étoile . . . tour à tour bleue et rose'. He has realised not only that *délice* and *tourment* are complementary, but also that his acute apprehension of both depends on the fact that his vision has a double nature. *Délice* and *tourment* are subjective: they are the two possible reactions of a complex spirit to a situation in which it stands to gain or lose everything. Woman may be both *reine* and *syrène*: but the real problem for Nerval is presented by the fact that his dual nature tends to see her as either one or the other, at any given moment; and as first one and then the other, over a period of time. By learning to accept her essential unity, he has learned also to accept his own. He is, moreover, in a position now to solve the problem of love, not only in relation to woman, but also in relation to God, for the difficulty of loving is essentially the same no matter what the object. With this solution in sight, 'El Desdichado' expresses a sense of harmony that is stronger than in any other of the sonnets. Though the other sonnets show an awareness of the need for reconciliation, their hints of possible unity are blurred by fears about identity or freedom, or simply by fears of the possible pain or violence involved in self-surrender. There can be no doubt that 'El Desdichado' records a discovery of the highest importance to the poet. It enables him to make sense of all his apparent contradictions, it offers a hope of the total reconciliation for which all these sonnets strive, and it saves the poet from despair, for he need no longer ask himself 'Suis-je le bon? suis-je le mauvais?' (*Aurélia*; I, 381).

In 'El Desdichado', we are told not only where salvation lies, but also what has been for Nerval the instrument of his salvation:

> Modulant tour à tour *sur la lyre d'Orphée* . . .

The *luth constellé* of the first quatrain reappears at the end of the sonnet, transfigured by the timelessness of myth. Orpheus went down into the Underworld to find Eurydice. He lost her a second time because, like Lusignan and like Psyche, he could not accept the conditions imposed on his love. In *Aurélia* (I, 385) Nerval begins the second part of his story with a reference to this legend: 'Eurydice! Eurydice! Une seconde fois perdue!' By the end of *Aurélia* he has come to terms with the conditions of love, and acquired some confidence in its reality and persistence. It is through that confidence that he feels himself to be saved. In 'El Desdichado', the same progress is made from the beginning of the first quatrain to the end of the final line, and the *lyre d'Orphée* is seen to be literally the key to the poet's release. It is through the making of poetry that he has gained his victory, as Orpheus with his music charmed the dangerous Sirens and the guardians of the Underworld. More precisely still, the synthesis he sought has been achieved *within the poem's structure*. The disparate elements have been placed side by side so that they might illuminate each other and find their true relation. Nerval has emerged from 'la nuit du tombeau' not merely by writing a poem, but by writing this particular poem, in which the apparent discords of his life have been used to create a harmonious and meaningful structure.

The assertions of a victory in 'El Desdichado' may perhaps be doubted by those who would prefer to accept the possibility that 'Artémis' may have been written later. That the poet was really 'vainqueur' has certainly been doubted by those who point to his suicide as proof of ultimate failure. Two answers to these objections suggest themselves. First, the sonnets of *Les Chimères*, in their final publication as a group, are arranged so that the greatest stress is on 'El Desdichado' and on 'Vers Dorés'; 'Artémis' is grouped with earlier sonnets in the centre of this edifice, and the poet does not appear to have wished the reader to regard it as his final word, even if it was the most recent. Secondly, we may assume that since Nerval was by nature subject to profound changes of mood, alternating (*tour à tour*) between elation and depression, even the conviction he speaks of at the end of *Aurélia*, and the victory of 'El Desdichado', would be powerless to protect him against a return of acute depression, such as he suffered immediately before his suicide. But the defeat of the man is not inconsistent with the victory of the poet, and even if 'Artémis' did follow 'El Desdichado', it cannot alter it. The present time in 'El Desdichado' is certainly dark: 'Je *suis* le téné-breux. . .'; but the poet has none the less made his 'descente aux enfers', and returned in triumph with a new-made harmony.

NOTES

INTRODUCTION

1. Passim, but see especially II, 719; and for Cain, II, 713–14.

2. Both 'Erythréa' and 'à Madame Aguado' are among the nine sonnets printed in the Pléiade edition under the heading *Autres Chimères* (I, 10–14). The text of 'Erythréa' is to be found on the manuscript which belonged to Paul Eluard; one sonnet, 'La Tête armée', was published in the *Poésies complètes* (Michel-Lévy, 1877); the other seven are on manuscripts in the Dumesnil de Gramont collection. These sonnets are interesting for the light they throw on Nerval's creative methods, since some of them offer alternative readings of *Les Chimères*. Perhaps even more interesting is the fact that the poet excluded from the final publication in 1854 those which do not contain variants of *Les Chimères*, and which might well have been published, since they stand on their own. He was evidently concerned to preserve the unity of his group of sonnets, and one must deduce that he did not feel that these particular sonnets belonged with the others. The fact that they were never published at all suggests further that he was not satisfied with them: and indeed, however interesting, they are decidedly less successful as poems than *Les Chimères*.

3. For example: P. Audiat, *L'Aurélia de Gérard de Nerval*, Champion, 1926, p. 115 (Audiat appears to include 'Myrtho' in this judgement); Jeanine Moulin, *Exégèses des Chimères*, Textes Littéraires Français, Giard et Droz, 1949, p. 50 (Mme Moulin here cites with approval N. Popa, *Introduction pour Les filles du feu*, éd. Champion); N. Popa, 'Le Thème et le Sentiment de la Mort chez Gérard de Nerval' (in *Mélanges de l'Ecole Roumaine en France*, 1925, Part 2): Popa sees 'Delfica' in much the same light.

4. A. Marie, *Gérard de Nerval, le Poète et l'Homme*, Hachette, 1955, p. 54 (2nd ed.; first published 1914). For a full discussion of the growth of Nerval's reputation, see the companion volume to this edition: N. Rinsler, *Gérard de Nerval*, Athlone Press, 1973.

5. Reprinted in O.C. I, 11–29. This Preface is a text of the greatest importance for the understanding of Nerval's work. It anticipates many of the themes of *Aurélia* and of *Les Chimères*, and indicates that the inspiration of the sonnets belongs to an earlier period than is usually suggested.

6. *Histoire du Romantisme*, Charpentier, 1874, p. 18. Gautier's analysis of Nerval's style offers a useful corrective to some of the wilder flights of later critics.

7. Cf. a similar remark made by Hugo in the preface to his *Odes* (1822): 'la poésie n'est pas dans la forme des idées, mais dans les idées elles-mêmes'.

8. In a letter to his father (31 May 1854; I, 1110) he remarks: 'je dois à la confiance des personnes qui m'ont soutenu de faire quelque chose de bon, peut-être d'utile'; the remark is interesting in its assumption that it is easier to write something 'good' than to be useful.

9. Ch. Baudelaire, *L'Art Romantique*, *Œuvres complètes* (ed. Crépet), Conrad, 1925, pp. 341 ff.

10. H. Heine, *Poëmes et Légendes*, *Œuvres complètes*, Calmann-Lévy, 1892, Préface, pp. vi–vii.

11. Th. Gautier, *Histoire du Romantisme*, p. 134; and Notice, *Faust et le Second Faust*, *Œuvres complètes de Gérard de Nerval*, Michel-Lévy, 1868, vol. i, p. v.

12. *Histoire du Romantisme*, p. 136.

13. H. de Régnier, 'Compte-Rendu' (of Rémy de Gourmont's 1897 edition of *Les Chimères*), *Mercure de France*, 1–XI–1897, 553.

14. A. Béguin, *Gérard de Nerval*, Librairie Stock, 1936, p. 92.

15. E. Aunos, *Gérard de Nerval et ses Énigmes*, Vidal, 1956, p. 65.

16. Y.–G. Le Dantec, Introduction, *Les Chimères*, Librairie de Médicis, 1947, p. 21.

17. G. Rouger, 'En Marge des Chimères', *Cahiers du Sud*, 292 (1948), 430–2.

18. *Cahiers du Sud*, 349 (1958), 446–9.

19. G. Le Breton, 'La Clé des *Chimères*: l'alchimie', *Fontaine*, no. 44 (1945), 441–60; 'L'Alchimie dans *Aurélia*: "Les Mémorables"', *Fontaine*, no. 45 (1945), 687–706. J. Richer, *Gérard de Nerval et les doctrines ésotériques*, Éditions du Griffon d'Or, 1947; *Nerval: expérience et création*, Hachette, 1963, is a more recent treatment of themes which Richer has studied in a long series of articles.

20. F. Constans, 'Ascendance mystique: existences mythiques', *Mercure de France*, 1–XI–1952, 449–61; 'Sibylles nervaliennes', *Revue des Sciences Humaines*, 91, (1958), 381–96; 94 (1959), 275–305; and many other articles.

21. L.-H. Sebillotte, *Le Secret de Gérard de Nerval*, Corti, 1948. Mauron, *Des métaphores obsédantes au mythe personnel*, Corti, 1963 (chapter IV deals with Nerval, and expands an article by Mauron published in 1949).

22. J.-P. Richard, *Poésie et profondeur*, Editions du Seuil, 1955 (chapter I).

23. L. Cellier, *Gérard de Nerval, l'homme et l'œuvre*, 'Connaissance des Lettres', Hatier-Boivin, 1956, p. 175. See also the same author's *Où en sont les recherches sur Gérard de Nerval?*, *Archives des Lettres modernes*, no. 3,

May 1957, p. 12. Nerval refers to *Robert le Diable* in *Voyage en Orient* (II, 459), and in *Petits Châteaux de Bohême* (I, 69).

24. C. G. Jung, *Psychological Reflections*, ed. Jolande Jacobi, Routledge and Kegan Paul, 1953, p. 266.

25. Cf. *Lettres à Jenny Colon*, I, 758: 'j'arrange volontiers ma vie comme un roman'. (These letters were given this title by the editors of the Pléiade edition; they are sometimes known as the *Lettres à Aurélia*; both titles are conjectural.)

26. Hugo uses the word in this way in his poem 'La Pente de la Rêverie' in *Feuilles d'Automne* (1831); some of the images in this poem can be traced to Nerval's translation of Schiller's ballad 'Der Taucher' (published in *Poésies allemandes*, 1830).

27. H. Heine, *Der Salon*, Hoffmann u. Campe, 1834, vol. i, p. 44. This text appeared in French in *De la France*, Renduel, 1834. Heine is here discussing the paintings of Decamps, who had been criticised for his 'unnatural' forms and colour-values. The French text has 'surnaturaliste' (and is so quoted by Baudelaire in his *Salon de 1846*); the German reads 'In der Kunst bin ich Supernaturalist'. Heine points out that art cannot find all its models in nature: the forms of architecture, for instance, come solely from man's mind. Decamps, he says, has painted 'ganz nach innerer Traumanschauung'; in the French version, 'il a, en peignant, été fidèle à la vérité fantastique et à l'intuition d'un rêve'. Heine's 'Traumanschauung' (dream-perception) is very close to Nerval's *rêverie*. What Nerval has to say about the possibility that his sonnets 'perdraient de leur charme à être expliqués' recalls an earlier passage in Heine's article on Decamps: 'J'attache surtout le plus grand prix à ce que le symbole, abstraction faite de sa signification secrète, charme en outre par lui-même les sens . . .'

28. Cf. a manuscript note (I, 421): 'S'entretenir d'idées pures et saines pour avoir des songes logiques'.

29. This fear may be reflected in the 'puits sombre' of 'Le Christ aux Oliviers', for the threshold of chaos is described as 'Spirale engloutissant les Mondes et les Jours'; the confusion of time and space is evidently frightening here. Heine remarks on the fear felt by human beings at the thought of death, which he says ought to be aroused by dream too, for in both 'ces deux béquilles, le temps et l'espace, leur manquent tout d'un coup' (*Schnabelewopski*, in *Reisebilder*; French version, *Tableaux de Voyage*, Renduel, 1834, re-issued 1853).

30. Arsène Houssaye, director of the review *L'Artiste* in which the first of the sonnets were published, and a close acquaintance of Nerval's, was one of the editors of an edition of Fontenelle's works, published in 1852. Nerval certainly knew the *Dialogues des Morts* of the Greek writer Lucian, whom Fontenelle was using as a model. Probably he knew them

best in the French translation of Bellin de Ballu (1789), though he claims to have read them in Greek at school (cf. *Voyage en Orient*; II, 83–4).

31. 'Que nous reste-t-il, à nous, les déïcides?'; 'Rolla' was published in *Revue des Deux Mondes*, 15 August 1833. Nerval quotes Musset's poem twice: in 'Le Bœuf gras' (1845; II, 1239) and in 'Les Dieux inconnus' (1845; II, 1244). In the preface to his *Odes* (1822), Hugo speaks of 'une vieille société, qui sort encore toute chancelante des saturnales de l'athéïsme et de l'anarchie'.

32. *Le Carnet de Dolbreuse*, Essai de lecture par Jean Richer, Athènes, 1967, no. 58, p. 44. This manuscript text proved difficult to decipher owing to Nerval's habit of making copious use of abbreviations and symbols of various kinds in his notebooks. Most of the passages which M. Richer has succeeded in reading appear to be sketches for a play (though at one stage Nerval may have intended to treat the subject as a novel). The work was never published, and probably never fully worked out; it appears in Nerval's own list of his *Œuvres complètes* under 'Ouvrages commencés ou inédits', with the note '2 vol.' (I, xxxiii). M. Richer argues convincingly that Nerval abandoned the work because it was too revealing of his attitude to his father. Many of the notes illuminate most interestingly Nerval's view of Romanticism and of the problems of his times.

33. Ibid., Préface, pp. 27–8.

34. Gautier believed that these poems were connected with Nerval's unhappy love for Jenny Colon, and speaks of them as if they were written about 1841 (*Histoire du Romantisme*, p. 149). He may have been referring only to the group published in 1853 in *Petits Châteaux de Bohême*, as he says that Nerval published his sonnets 'plus tard sous le titre de *Vers dorés*'.

35. It was the lame god Hephaestus who, at the command of Zeus (Jupiter), forged the chains and rings that bound Prometheus to his rock. Hephaestus, the lame god of fire whom the Romans called Vulcan, appears in 'Horus' as Kneph, 'le dieu des volcans' (see commentary on 'Horus').

36. In a review of Leon Halévy's translations of Greek drama; the review was published in *La Presse*, 5 October 1846, and is reprinted in O.C. II, 701. Nerval's quotation is from Halévy.

37. It has such significance also, as a passage of *L'Imagier de Harlem* shows (O.C. V, 137): when Coster almost succeeds, through his love for her, in freeing Alilah from her bondage to the devil, she compares him to Prometheus, whose 'fire' here is obviously the fire of love, like the fires of the volcano in 'Myrtho':

O paroles d'espoir! . . . ai-je bien entendu!
Voilà l'homme, voilà mon génie attendu!
Il n'a douté de rien, et son âme est montée
Jusqu'au ciel, pour ravir le feu de Prométhée.

Nerval refers obliquely to the punishment that is likely to overtake those who claim dominion over the element of fire, in his article 'Le Boulevard du Temple—Aujourd'hui' (*L'Artiste*, 1844); Daguerre's Diorama had recently burned down, and Nerval had watched the fire, 'cet élément perfide', at work: 'le *Diorama* voisin (l'ancien) s'abîmait dans les flammes. Je l'ai vu flamber et crouler en dix minutes . . . Le feu s'était vengé ainsi de ce pauvre Daguerre, qui, pendant ce temps lui dérobait ses secrets et faisait travailler les rayons du soleil à des planches en manière noire' (O.C. VIII, 71).

38. Maud Bodkin, *Archetypal Patterns in Poetry*, O.U.P., 2nd ed., 1951, p. 286 (first published 1931).

39. Fabre d'Olivet, 'Etudes sur la poésie tragique des Grecs'. This article was published in Nerval's own journal, *Le Monde Dramatique*, 1835, vol. i, 210–12. Fabre d'Olivet himself translated Byron's *Cain* (see commentary on 'Antéros').

40. Bodkin, op. cit., p. 259.

41. Sainte-Beuve, *Pensées de Joseph Delorme*, XII, *Œuvres*, Lemerre, 1879, vol. i, pp. 208–9.

42. Nerval seems to have been rejected because of his condemnation of Malherbe. Sainte-Beuve became so absorbed in his study of the Pléiade that he did not finish his essay in time to compete; he published in 1828 his influential *Tableau historique et critique de la poésie française . . . au XVIe siècle*, in which Ronsard is compared favourably with Malherbe. The prize was won jointly by Saint-Marc Girardin and Philarète Chasles, both of whom see Ronsard as deviating from the mainstream of French tradition, to which Malherbe returned.

43. Cf. 'Sonnet—Imité de Wordsworth', ed. cit., p. 171.

44. 'Du Bartas', *Revue des Deux Mondes*, Jan.-March 1842, 549–75.

45. H. Meschonnic, 'Essai sur la poétique de Nerval', *Europe*, 353, 1958, 10–33. Very little critical attention has been given to Nerval's poetic method; this study is perhaps the only one which really illuminates the subject.

46. See the companion volume to this edition (cf. note 4).

47. Hélène Tuzet, 'L'image du Soleil Noir', *Revue des Sciences Humaines* 88, October-December 1957, 479–502.

48. There is an echo here of Descartes's 'troisième maxime' (*Discours de la méthode*, Troisième Partie): 'de tâcher toujours plutôt à me vaincre que la fortune, et à changer mes désirs que l'ordre du monde, et

généralement de m'accoutumer à croire qu'il n'y a rien qui soit
entièrement en notre pouvoir que nos pensées . . .'

49. *Le Carnet de Dolbreuse*, no. 206, p. 59.

COMMENTARIES

Foreword

50. J. Guillaume, '*Les Chimères' de Nerval, Edition critique*, Académie de
Langue et de Littérature Françaises, Bruxelles, 1966.

51. *Times Literary Supplement*, 21 March 1968, p. 289.

52. *Histoire du Romantisme*, p. 132.

53. *Voyage en Orient*, II, 64.

54. *Le Carnet de Dolbreuse*, no. 202, p. 58. Cf. also no. 212, p. 59.

55. L. Bisson expresses a similar view with regard to Hugo's *Feuilles
d'Automne* (Blackwell's French Texts, 1948, Introduction, p. ix).

Le Christ aux Oliviers

56. See Albert Béguin, 'Le *Songe* de Jean-Paul et Victor Hugo', *Revue de
Littérature comparée*, 1934, 703–13. See also Cl. Pichois, *L'Image de Jean-
Paul Richter dans les lettres françaises*, Corti, 1963, chapter VII, 'Le "Songe"
dans la littérature romantique', pp. 254–93.

57. The quotation in translation is from Madame de Staël's *De
l'Allemagne*, Les Grands Ecrivains de la France, Hachette, 1958-60, vol.
iii, p. 288.

58. Nerval makes *orbite* masculine, as does Madame de Staël's trans-
lation. Some dictionaries still record it as being of either gender, but it is
now generally regarded as a feminine noun. A. Béguin in his article
(see note 56) incorrectly gives 'une orbite Vaste, noire . . .' in his quota-
tion from 'Le Christ aux Oliviers'; so does the Pléiade edition.

59. Nerval refers to this passage of *Paradise Lost* in 'Paradoxe et Vérité'
(I, 431), which was first published in *L'Artiste*, 2 June 1844: 'Philo-
sophie! ta lumière, comme celle des enfers de Milton, ne sert qu'à
rendre les ténèbres visibles'.

60. The 'puits sombre' and the rainbow, as well as the 'sphères vaga-
bondes', are derived directly from the German text; these phrases are
omitted in Madame de Staël's translation.

61. Curiously, the Greeks very often spoke of Iris's scarf as if it only
appeared when the gods required her for some errand of mischief. She
thus acquires an association with discord which is quite opposed to the
Biblical image of the rainbow. Nerval seems not to have been worried by
these conflicting associations; at any rate, the rainbow is evidently a
symbol of hope in this poem, though it may be more ambiguous in
'Horus'.

62. *Poésies allemandes . . . morceaux choisis et traduits par M. Gérard*, 1830. The Introduction to this volume is reprinted in O.C. I, pp. 34–55. It is one of the rare documents in which Nerval expresses his opinions about literature.

63. The Diorama was a kind of peepshow invented by Bouton and Daguerre. Nerval's article is a review of its reopening performance, a representation of the Deluge (*L'Artiste*, 15 September 1844).

64. There is a curious echo of this 'silent sentinel' image in *Aurélia* (I, 407), where Nerval speaks of a fellow-patient who was recommended to his care by Dr Blanche, and in whose plight he found the means to his own salvation through patience and affection for another human being. Nerval describes the young man as 'ancien soldat d'Afrique . . . il ne pouvait ni voir ni parler . . . un être indéfinissable, taciturne et patient, assis comme un sphinx aux portes suprêmes de l'existence . . .' See commentary on *Aurélia* in the companion volume to this edition.

65. Nerval comments in 'Quintus Aucler' (II, 1211) on Dupont de Nemours's theory that 'L'homme, les bêtes et les plantes ont une *monade* immortelle . . .'. The term *monade*, as Nerval remarks, is used by Leibnitz. It signifies the irreducible principle of life, and is thus equivalent to Nerval's 'haleine immortelle'. Nerval transcribes (II, 1198) passages from Aucler dealing with similar notions, and correctly traces their origin back to the Orphic cosmogonies (there is further discussion of these ideas in Nerval's 'Cagliostro'; II, 1170–84). Orphism arose in the sixth century B.C., and profoundly influenced both Pythagorean and Platonic philosophy; its central symbol is the god Dionysus (Iacchus) who represents the divine element in man; his resurrection is like that of Christ, and the image of Orpheus was used by the early Christians as a cipher for the Christ-figure.

66. Lucifer was seen by the Romantics in general as a Romantic rebel; see Introduction, and commentary on 'Antéros'.

67. Latin *satelles*, 'escort, guard'; *satellites* carries an implication of subservience—'henchmen'.

68. Cybele was originally a hermaphrodite deity; at an early stage in her cult, she became a female, and the severed male organs of the hermaphrodite were laid in the earth. From them grew a pomegranate tree, which impregnated a nymph, who gave birth to the boy Atys. Atys was thus the son of a deity, but born to a virgin, like Christ. When he grew up, Cybele fell in love with him, but he castrated himself and died to preserve his chastity.

69. First published by Renduel, 1835; p. 164. Nerval refers to Fichte in *Les Nuits d'Octobre* (I, 106). Heine's notes on the German philosophers find many echoes in Nerval's writings.

70. Cf. Matthew, xxvii, 51. In *Voyage en Orient* (II, 89) Nerval records

(from his English source, Edward Dodwell) that a priest of Apollo was struck dead by a 'tremblement de terre' when, at the moment of Christ's death, he cried aloud that 'un nouveau Dieu venait de naître, dont la puissance égalerait celle d'Apollon, mais qui finirait pourtant par lui céder'. There is an echo of the prophetic trembling of the earth in 'Delfica', in 'Myrtho', and in 'Horus', where it is associated with the death of the god Kneph.

71. Ammon (Amun, or Amun-Re) was originally a sky-god, later established at Thebes as king of the gods of the Middle Kingdom of Egypt. The Greeks recognised him as equivalent to Zeus, and called Thebes 'Diospolis', the city of Zeus. The oracle of Jupiter-Ammon in the Oasis of Sïwah in outer Libya 'ranked with Delphi and Dodona as one of the three great oracles of the Greek world' (*Cambridge Ancient History*, vol. 6, 1927, p. 377). In 332 B.C., Alexander visited the oracle and there proclaimed himself the son of Ammon, in order to consolidate his power in Egypt. In the *Carnet de Notes du Voyage en Orient* (II, 719) Nerval places the names 'Ammon Zeus' side by side. In the preface to *Les Filles du Feu* he quotes Dumas's introduction to 'El Desdichado', in which Dumas mentions 'la route brûlée d'Alexandrie à Ammon' (I, 150).

72. Cf. *Voyage en Orient*: 'Adam, pétri de limon et dépositaire d'une âme captive' (II, 561); '[les] enfants de Sem pétris du limon de la terre' (II, 579).

73. First published in the *Revue de Paris*, November 1851, and included in the volume *Les Illuminés*, published in 1852.

Vers Dorés

74. 'Le pythagorisme de Nerval et la source des "Vers dorés" ', *La Tour Saint-Jacques* 13–14 (janvier-avril 1958), 79–87.

75. The original version of this sonnet ('Pensée antique', 1845) has 'ta *royauté* dispose', which Le Breton (see note 74) derives from Delisle's reference to man's desire to see himself as 'le roi de la nature'. The substitution of *liberté* links this verse more closely with the notion of the 'libre penseur'; but Nerval may simply have wished to improve the sound of the verse; that is probably the reason for the other variant (l. 6): *chaque plante* in the original version was replaced by *chaque fleur*.

76. *Pascal's Apology for Religion*, H. F. Stewart, Cambridge University Press, 1948, pp. 49–50. Stewart numbers these *Pensées* 147–9; in editions which follow Brunschvicg's classification, these are nos. 347, 348, 339. Nerval mentions Pascal in *Les Nuits d'Octobre* (I, 107).

77. In a review of *Émile ou le Chien du Contrebandier*, published in *La Presse*, 4 August 1845; see O.C. II, 660–1. The Cuvier who is discussed later the same month (ibid., 666) is not the same person, though Nerval seems to be unaware of the fact. The studies on the intelligence of animals

were made by Frédéric Georges Cuvier; the studies of fossil remains and comparative anatomy by his more famous elder brother, Baron Georges Cuvier. Nerval mentions him as early as 1841 in an article 'De la Propriété littéraire' (O.C. I, 193) in the triumvirate 'Cuvier, Walter Scott, ou Chateaubriand'; and in 1850 he noted with approval, in Goethe's house in Weimar, that medallions by the sculptor David in Goethe's collection included Cuvier and Chateaubriand, as well as other French poets and writers (II, 799). Cuvier's presence among the poets may seem strange; but Balzac in *La Peau de Chagrin* (1831) refers to Cuvier's studies of fossil remains found at Montmartre (to which Nerval also refers in *Les Nuits d'Octobre*, 1852, I, 82; and in *Promenades et Souvenirs*, 1854, I, 122), and he remarks: 'Cuvier n'est-il pas le plus grand poète de notre siècle? . . . notre immortel naturaliste a reconstruit des mondes avec des os blanchis, a rebâti comme Cadmus des cités avec des dents . . .' —which recalls the hero of 'Antéros'.

78. See for instance S. A. Rhodes, *Gérard de Nerval*, Peter Owen, 1952, pp. 234–5.

79. André Breton, *Manifestes du Surréalisme*, Pauvert, 1962, pp. 362–3.

Delfica

80. The first of these documents also has a sonnet entitled 'à Madame Aguado' (I, 13–14) whose final lines offer another version of the second tercet of 'Delfica:'

> Cependant la prêtresse au visage vermeil,
>
> Est endormie encor sous l'arche du soleil.
>
> Et rien n'a dérangé le sévère portique.

A variant of 'à Madame Aguado', with the title 'Erythréa' (I, 14), appears on a manuscript in the collection of Paul Eluard.

81. Vergil's Fourth Eclogue is sometimes given the title 'Pollio'; it was written during Pollio's consulship (40 B.C.) and the child is presumed to be Pollio's son. Nerval's quotations are from lines 4 and 6:

> Ultima Cumæi venit iam carminis ætas . . .
>
> iam redit et Virgo, redeunt Saturnia regna . . .

'Now is come the last age of the song of Cumae . . . Now the Virgin returns, the reign of Saturn returns . . .' The virgin, according to some editors, is Astraea (Justice), who was the last of the immortals to leave the earth.

82. Epigraphs were fashionable among Romantic poets, and Hugo, for instance, seems to have gone through the proofs of *Feuilles d'Automne* adding epigraphs to poems which had obviously been conceived without them. This fashion was virtually discarded after 1845, and Hugo removed the epigraphs from later editions of *Feuilles d'Automne*. Nerval's epigraphs. which have a real connection with the poems to which he attached them,

were retained in *Petits Châteaux de Bohême* in 1853, and except in the case of 'Delfica', in 1854.

83. Gilbert Rouger, 'En Marge des Chimères', *Cahiers du Sud*. 292 (1948), 430–2.

84. See note 70.

85. In *Sylvie, suive de Léo Burckart et d'Aurélia*, ed. H. Clouard, Éditions du Rocher, 1946, p. 157. M. Jean Richer has announced a critical edition of this play, based on the published text and the original version accepted by the theatre management; the two versions are compared in J. Richer, 'Nerval et ses deux *Léo Burckart*', *Mercure de France*, 1–XII–49. 645–78. See also commentary on 'Antéros'.

86. The 'grotte' recalls 'la grotte où nage la sirène' of 'El Desdichado'. and there may well be some confusion of the two images, suggesting that the 'chanson d'amour' of 'Delfica' may be a song of a darker kind than at first appears. Nerval also mentions in *Voyage en Orient* (II, 316) that he saw 'la grotte d'où sortit le fameux dragon qui était prêt à dévorer la fille du roi de Beyrouth, lorsque saint Georges le perça de sa lance'.

87. Similar ideas are discussed in another of the pieces in *Les Illuminés*, 'Jacques Cazotte', first published in 1845, some months before 'Delfica' appeared. A group of texts dealing with related subjects is published in II, 1215–44; the majority of these date from 1844–5, and in them Nerval comments on most of the mystical or illuminist doctrines which were current at the time.

88. 'Elle imprimait ses dents d'ivoire dans l'écorce d'un citron' (I, 286). In the fragment known as *Voyage d'Italie—Panorama*, there is another reference to this incident: 'La fille blonde qui mange des citrons... Oh fille blasée' (I, 425).

89. A description of the Grotte du chien, and of other caves around Naples, is to be found in F. M. Misson, *Nouveau Voyage d'Italie*, La Haye, 1731, vol. ii, p. 64. It was, in my view, from this work that Nerval took the enigmatic inscription which he uses to describe Pandora (see note 109).

90. The sycamore is in itself ambiguous. The tree known by this name in Northern Europe is the sycamore maple, a very large timber tree allied to the true maple. The Egyptian or Oriental sycamore is a kind of fig-tree which grows in Egypt and Syria (the word sycamore is derived from the Greek names for fig and mulberry); in the *Carnet de Notes du Voyage en Orient* (II, 715) it is mentioned in what appear to be notes for a description of a palace garden: 'sycomores. Figuiers'. Nerval refers (II, 248) to the tradition that the Holy Family rested beneath a sycamore on the Flight into Egypt. The *sycomore* of 'Delfica' is thus both a northern and a southern tree, like the *mûriers* of 'à J-y Colonna';

Nerval saw mulberry trees growing beside olive trees in Greece (II, 76).

91. The first version of 'Horus' (see note 105) has *dort* instead of *meurt*.

92. Nerval recognised that the multiplicity of strange beliefs current in his time was due to a nostalgia like his own, and not to a genuine scepticism. In 'Les Dieux inconnus' (1845) he remarked that 'ce ne sont pas les dieux qui manquent', and after surveying some of them, he comments: 'Criez donc après cela au positivisme, à l'incrédulité de l'époque!' (II, 1240, 1244).

Myrtho

93. Cf. Vigny, 'La Dryade':

> Ida! j'adore Ida, la légère bacchante:
>
> Ses *cheveux noirs*, *mêlés* de *grappes* et d'acanthe . . .

94. A curious echo of this image appears in Rémy de Gourmont, who edited *Les Chimères* in 1897. In his *Litanies de la Rose* (which is itself like a protracted echo of 'Artémis', 'Rose au cœur violet, fleur de sainte Gudule') he writes: 'Rose hortensia, ô banales délices des âmes distinguées, rose néo-chrétienne, ô rose hortensia, tu nous dégoûtes de Jésus, fleur hypocrite, fleur du silence'.

95. In *Journal d'un Poète*, ed. F. Baldensperger, Scholartis Press, 1928, pp. 196–7.

96. Nerval refers to Julian's dying words in 'Quintus Aucler' (II, 1208): 'Tu m'as vaincu, Nazaréen!'

97. *Isis*, I, 301–3. Cf. also II, 1207: 'Iacchus-Iésus, plus connu en France sous le nom de Christ'; and Isis's words in *Aurélia* (I, 399): 'Je suis la même que Marie . . .'

98. In *La Pandora*, the poet accuses the woman of poisoning the air: ' "Ne sais-tu pas qu'on ne peut plus respirer ici? L'air est infecté de tes poisons . . . De l'air! de l'air! Nous périssons!" ' But he also is guilty, and is punished: 'Une sensation douloureuse . . . dans ma gorge . . . Je me trouvai étranglé. On me trancha la tête . . .' (I, 354–5). In *Les Nuits d'Octobre*, the dreamer is similarly punished for having desired La Femme Mérinos, whose description is remarkably like that of Pandora as the poet saw her in his dreams: he suffers a violent headache ('on me brise la tête à grands coups de marteau') and 'il respire avec peine' (I, 104–6). There are further links between *La Pandora* and 'Myrtho': Pandora with her 'sourire divin' is called 'enchanteresse' by the poet (I, 356), recalling the 'divine enchanteresse' of 'Myrtho'; and the courtesan Impéria (see p. 89) appears in *La Pandora* (I, 355).

99. Nerval's translations of Heine's poems appeared in the *Revue des Deux Mondes*, 15 July 1848 (*Nordsee*) and 15 September 1848 (*Intermezzo*); but he had been working on them since at least 1840 (see I, 871).

100. O.C. V, 89, n. 79; 129, n. 46.

101. Cf. *Carnet de Notes du Voyage en Orient*, II, 719; Nerval here places the names of gods alongside their equivalents in other religions, and among them 'Φta Hephaistos'. Ptah is equivalent to Kneph in Egyptian mythology, and Vulcan's Greek name was Hephaistos.

102. *Voyage en Orient*, II, 81; II, 1293, n. 13. The early chapters of the *Voyage* are haunted by the image of Venus. They were first published in *l'Artiste* in 1844–5, that is, at the same period as 'Le Christ aux Oliviers', 'Vers Dorés', and 'Delfica'. Significantly, the description of 'l'épouse légère du boiteux Vulcain' was omitted from the text when it appeared in volume form in 1851: it bears too closely on Nerval's private mythology.

103. François Constans notes a resemblance to the description of Atlas in the *Æneid* (IV, 251); see 'Sibylles nervaliennes', II, *Revue des Sciences Humaines*, 94 (1959), 275–92.

104. The scarf of Iris has, however, associations with discord (see note 61). It is perhaps deliberately ambiguous in this final tercet, symbolising both the possibility of rebirth and the discord between Isis and Kneph (and presumably also between Horus and Kneph) which must precede it.

105. The sonnet 'à Louise d'Or Reine' is reproduced here (from Guillaume, op. cit., p. 104), since the variants are both complex and significant:

> Le vieux père en tremblant ébranlait l'univers
> Isis la mère enfin se leva sur sa couche,
> Fit un geste de haine à son époux farouche,
> Et l'ardeur d'autrefois brilla dans ses yeux verts.
>
> "Regardez le! dit-elle, il dort ce vieux pervers,
> "Tous les frimats du monde ont passé par sa bouche
> "Prenez garde à son pied, éteignez son œil louche,
> "C'est le roi des volcans et le Dieu des hivers!"
>
> "L'aigle a déjà passé: Napoléon m'appelle;
> "J'ai revêtu pour lui la robe de Cybèle,
> "C'est mon époux Hermès, et mon frère Osiris;
>
> "La Déesse avait fui sur sa conque dorée;
> "La mer nous renvoyait son image adorée
> "Et les cieux rayonnaient sous l'écharpe d'Iris!

106. Nerval's earliest poems are full of the legend of Napoleon, whom he associated with his own father's military career. But his admiration for this most splendid of Romantic heroes had vanished by 1840, when he wrote a poem ('Napoléon', subtitled 'Décembre 1840—pour le retour des cendres') on the occasion of the transfer of Napoleon's ashes to the Panthéon. This fact may help us to date the first conception of 'Horus',

for 'à Louise d'Or Reine' almost certainly antedates 'Napoléon'. Some phrases of 'Napolèon' resemble another of the sonnets on the same manuscript as 'à Louise d'Or Reine': 'à Madame Sand'. These facts point again to the probability that most of *Les Chimères* were conceived before 1840–1.

107. Weill's account of his visit to Nerval at Dr Blanche's clinic, early in 1841, is reprinted in the notes to the *Correspondance* (I, 1384–5; Lettre 81, n. 2).

Antéros

108. See, in *Voyage en Orient*, the chapter entitled 'L'Entrevue' (II. 587–90); in the *Correspondance*, letters from the Middle East dated 1842–3; and *Aurélia*, I, 385–6: this passage is discussed in the Introduction.

Artémis

109. The latter manuscript contains also a quotation from the enigmatic inscription 'Aelia Laelia', quoted in full by Misson in his *Nouveau Voyage d'Italie* (see note 89), and used by Nerval in *La Pandora* to describe the enigma of woman. There is something of the classical enigma in the form of 'Artémis', especially in the constant presentation of alternatives (see p. 107–8).

110. J. Richer, *Nerval: expérience et création*, Hachette, 1963, p. 582 ff.

111. Cf. the description of Judas ('Le Christ aux Oliviers') as 'le *seul*'.

112. In 'Fantaisie', which was first published in 1832, and republished at intervals until it appeared in *Petits Châteaux de Bohême* (1853), the themes of time, love and loss are already present, but set in a context of French history and a French landscape from which *Les Chimères* departs: to return, however, eventually, in what may be the last of the sonnets, 'El Desdichado'.

113. The theme of 'ressemblances', which begins in *Fantaisie*, is one of the threads that runs right through Nerval's work: it is an important element in *Octavie*, *Corilla*, and *Sylvie*, and in his study of Restif de la Bretone, 'Les Confidences de Nicolas'.

114. Nerval is here adapting the *Golden Ass* of Apuleius. The 'robe en taffetas changeant' of the vision in *Aurélia* is also echoed in *Isis*: 'sa robe aux reflets indécis passe, selon le mouvement de ses plis, de la blancheur la plus pure au jaune de safran . . .' (I, 301).

115. Stewart, op. cit., p. 79, Pensée No. 234 (Brunschvicg no. 242).

116. Louis Réau, *Iconographie de l'art chrétien*, Presses universitaires 1958–9; vol. iii—'Iconographie des saints'. Sainte Gudule appears with a lantern in Gérard David's *Death of the Virgin* (1515), and in Joos van Cleve's *Death of Mary* (1520), both of which Nerval may have seen when he visited the Pinakothek in Munich.

117. The church, in the Place Ste Gudule, was formerly known as the Collegiate Church of St Michael and St Gudule, but is now generally known as the Cathedral of St Michael.

118. Maxime du Camp describes a drawing by Nerval in his possession in which the central figure was 'une femme géante, nimbée de sept étoiles, qui appuie des pieds sur le globe, où rampe le dragon et qui symbolise à la fois Diane, Sainte Rosalie et Jenny Colon' (*Souvenirs littéraires*, Hachette, 1882–3; vol. ii, p. 162). This description recalls Baroque statues representing the Virgin standing upon a globe around which a serpent is entwined; sometimes the crescent moon is beside her feet—which seems to reinforce her likeness to Diana. The monumental pulpit of Ste Gudule has a statue of the Virgin of this kind. For examples of this iconography, see plates in *Baroque Sculpture*, ed. H. Busch and B. Lohse, Batsford, 1965, pp. 132, 150.

119. Published in *L'Artiste*, 7 July 1844. The article is a review of the actress Rachel's farewell benefit performance in Racine's *Phèdre*; it is reprinted in O.C. II, 589–90.

120. For the image of Venus, see commentary on 'Horus' and note 102. Venus is also described (II, 82) as one of the 'vierges saintes', and as 'la Vénus des abîmes'; as 'sainte de l'abîme' she obviously has links with 'Artémis'.

121. See Introduction for discussion of the significance of Arthémise.

122. O.C. V, 137–8. This play is deeply concerned with the problem of love between man and woman, and the figure of Alilah reflects all Nerval's fears and hopes when faced with the possibility of loving: there is no middle way; love leads either to heaven or to hell, and to consent to love is to risk everything.

123. François Constans, 'Artémis ou les Fleurs du Désespoir', *Revue de Littérature comparée*, 1934, 337–71.

124. L.-H. Sebillotte, *Le Secret de Gérard de Nerval*, Corti, 1948.

125. For the image of Prometheus, see Introduction. During his periodic bouts of depression, Nerval suffered bitterly from his inability to trust and love even his closest friends. He describes himself in such a mood of depression ('Madame et Souveraine'; I, 43):

> Méfiant comme un rat, trompé par trop de gens,
>
> Ne croyant nullement aux amitiés sincères . . .

It is a state in which he is deprived of the consolations of his *chimères*. The end of depression brings a renewed belief in love: 'J'étais si heureux de sentir mon cœur capable d'un amour nouveau! . . .' (*Aurélia*; I, 360). The lack of feeling associated with depression caused him more pain than did emotional suffering; in his study of Heine (O.C. I, 89) he welcomes the sufferings of love which Heine describes: 'Qui ne voudrait souffir ainsi? Ne rien sentir, voilà le supplice . . .'

El Desdichado

126. In vol. I of the Pléiade edition (first published 1952); 'Artémis' is still so described in the 3rd edition, 1960.

127. In the original version of 'Le Monstre Vert' (in *Le Diable Vert*, 1850); see 'Note essentielle,' I, 1295. (This passage was omitted from the publication in volume form of *Contes et Facéties*, 1852.) The title alone of Lesage's novel would have sufficed to attract Nerval's attention; see note 133.

128. A. Kies, 'Une source d'*El Desdichado*: *Le Diable boiteux* de Lesage', *Les Lettres romanes*, November 1953, 357.

129. *Voyage en Orient*, II, 136. Dürer's 'angel' is the figure in his engraving 'Melancholia', which fascinated both Gautier and Nerval. Describing a vision which he saw when in a state of depression, Nerval compares its central figure to 'l'Ange de la *Mélancolie*, d'Albrecht Dürer' (*Aurélia*; I, 362).

130. See commentary on 'Delfica' and note 88.

131. The Lombard manuscript and the version published in *Le Mousquetaire* have 'le pampre à la vigne s'allie'. The version of 1854 is clearly superior, as well as being nearer to the text of *Sylvie*. The association of rose and vine is found twice more in *Sylvie*, in the description of Loisy ('vingt chaumières dont la vigne et les roses grimpantes festonnent les murs'; I, 252), and in the final chapter where the narrator, in the inn at Dammartin, opens his window 'encadrée de vigne et de roses' (I, 272). The Paul Eluard manuscript (title, 'Le Destin') has a note against the eighth line: 'Jardin du Vatican'. In *La Pandora*, the dreamer finds himself 'à Rome sous les berceaux fleuris de la treille du Vatican, où la belle Impéria trônait à la table sacrée, entourée d'un conclave de cardinaux'. The associations here (see commentary on *La Pandora* in the companion volume to this edition) are less pleasant than in *Octavie*, where the poet waits for the English girl, after his troubled night and melancholy dawn, 'pensif sous une treille'; the thought of Octavie had saved him from 'la nuit du tombeau', though he ultimately rejects her as he does, in his dream, Impéria.

The union of the Valois and the Mediterranean was a constant dream of Nerval's (see commentaries on 'Delfica' and 'Artémis'). Other examples occur in *Sylvie* (I, 256–7, 259).

132. *Des Inédits de Gérard de Nerval*, ed. Gisèle Marie, Editions Mercure de France, 1939, p. 39.

133. For example II, 35, 43. Byron is of course also associated with Greece, where he died. Nerval, in his study of Heine, calls Byron 'fils du soleil' (O.C. I, 78), which links him with Phébus. Finally, like Bìron le Boiteux, like Kneph and like Nerval's father, the poet Byron was lame.

134. There is an odd parallel here with a line of 'Antéros': 'Il m'a marqué le front de sa lèvre irritée'. The 'implacable rougeur' of Cain seems to echo 'Mon front est rouge encor du baiser de la reine . . .' Both marks are the seal of a destiny. The mark on Cain's forehead was placed there by God to protect him from the vengeance of his fellow-men—but not with a kiss: 'de sa lèvre irritée' appears to be Nerval's invention.

135. See commentary on 'Myrtho'.

136. A note in Nerval's hand on the Eluard manuscript confirms the link between this final line and the first tercet. Against *la fée* he has written 'Mélusine'. Mélusine was the wife of Lusignan; she bore the tail of a serpent on one day of every week, and forbade him to visit her on that day. Suspecting that she had a lover, Lusignan disobeyed her, and she vanished for ever. She returns, the legend says, to circle the castle towers, crying piteously, when the lords of Lusignan are dying: hence the 'cris de la fée'. Nerval quotes Heine in his study of *Nordsee* (O.C. I, 78–9): 'il s'écrie, à propos de Lusignan, amant de Mélusine: "Heureux homme dont la maîtresse n'était serpent qu'à moitié!" . . .'

137. The first sign of a shift from a preoccupation with the nature of the external world to a questioning of the poet's own nature comes perhaps in 'Antéros': here the duality of Abel and Cain seems to be thought of in terms of a contrast between loved and unloved which is like the contrasts of the first tercet of 'El Desdichado'. This may be further evidence for a later date for 'Antéros' (see commentary on this sonnet).